Federal Aid and Catholic Schools

Federal Aid
and
Catholic Schools

edited by Daniel Callahan

HELICON

Baltimore—Dublin

Helicon Press, Inc.
1120 N. Calvert St.
Baltimore, Maryland 21202

Library of Congress Catalog Card Number 64-16132

PRINTED IN THE UNITED STATES OF AMERICA BY
GARAMOND/PRIDEMARK PRESS, BALTIMORE, MARYLAND

Contents

APPENDIX

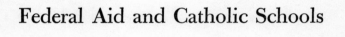

Federal Aid and Catholic Schools

DANIEL CALLAHAN

Into the Briar Patch

Some months ago, when my colleagues and I thought to put together a collection of articles on federal aid to Catholic schools, we were at once stymied. Precisely what, we asked ourselves, is the central problem? But this question was no sooner asked than rejected. At one time, it might have been possible to talk in terms of an overriding issue: that would have been the constitutionality of aid to religious schools. We now believe that the legal question is only one of many, no doubt still of central importance but surrounded by such a tangle of social, cultural, historical and educational issues that it can no longer be considered in isolation.

The question we now put to ourselves is: How can one find a path through this briar patch? And how, before one starts looking, can one persuade the other members of the search party to leave their traditional weapons outside: sabers (for we like to slash one another); spiked maces (for we enjoy at times brute force); shibboleths (which can be flung at will); scaling ladders and hot lead (the former to surmount any "wall of separation," the latter to repel those who try).

The imagery, I'm afraid, is not overdone. For well over a hundred years Americans have struggled over the place of the religious school in the American educational system. Time and again, the courts have had to render decisions on this or that point of contention. One generation after another has found something to argue about, and ours is no exception.

Yet there is a difference, or rather there are many differences. Today Catholics are coming to see, by and large, that the old ideal of every Catholic child in a Catholic school is impossibly utopian. Today non-Catholics are gradually conceding—again, by and large—that the religious school is here to stay and that it is a significant part of American education (whether desirable or not). Today all Americans, whether Catholic or non-Catholic, are beginning to admit that, taken as a whole, American education suffers many glaring weaknesses.

However wrongly motivated, the launching by the Soviet Union of Sputnik I in 1957 set off a vast wave of panic among educators, politicians, and the public at large. That panic, of course, died down in time—only to be replaced by the more serious awareness that, if we lack engineers, we lack something still more important: schools prepared to cope with the huge mass of children in our society who know nothing but poverty, discrimination and broken homes; schools able to encourage and assist the very bright student; schools capable of paying teachers decent wages and attracting the best possible candidates. Even if, gruesomely, the thrust of a rocket booster could conceivably determine the destiny of our civilization, we are still dealing with possibilities. But in the general quality of American education, we are dealing with immediate realities; and they are depressing. It is considerations such as these which ought to be kept well in mind when approaching the narrower province of federal aid to Catholic schools.

Yet in what I term the "narrower province" there are

many new forces which have also served to re-shape the old debate. Faced with a growing shortage of priests, nuns, and brothers, the Catholic schools have been forced to rely increasingly on lay teachers. This means, not surprisingly, increased expenses. A booming Catholic population has necessitated a vast and rapid building program—not to increase the percentage of children in Catholic schools, but just to stay even. That means more expenses. The schools themselves, to cap the story, require facilities and equipment hardly dreamed of even a few decades ago. Still more expenses. Hence even apart from the implications, say, of a large program of federal spending for the public schools (with higher taxes to be borne by all), the Catholic schools are facing a financial crisis.

Apart from that crisis, less observable undercurrents are at work, some of a very contradictory nature. Despite the belief of many non-Catholics, there is every reason to believe the assertion of the clergy that it is the Catholic parent, and not the priest or bishop, who provides the loudest part of the clamor for more and better schools (though this is perhaps the result of years of persuasion). Almost every Catholic school is overcrowded and can boast a long waiting list. At the same time, one can find more and more Catholic parents who have consciously rejected the parochial school for their children. Many, to be sure, do so because of indifference to religious education. Others want what they believe to be the better secular education which the public schools give (though whether, on the whole, it is better is debatable). But a surprising number of parents reject the parochial school because they believe their children will receive a bad, or at least inferior, religious education, one which will be positively harmful to their child's Catholic faith. They are unwilling, in brief, to accept a second-rate secular education in a parochial school for the sake of gaining a fourth-rate religious education. Though this latter group is still small, I have no doubt it is growing rapidly.

For all this diversity in Catholic parental attitudes, there is no less variety in the views of Catholic educators. At present there is a developing debate whether the parochial schools should be gradually abandoned in favor of Catholic high schools, thus enabling the Church to concentrate its efforts. Now and then, one can hear a suggestion that the parochial schools should consciously select only the most promising students, thus making the schools a training ground for potential Catholic leaders. Again, one can find an occasional bold voice urging the American hierarchy to cease worrying so much about the schools, to relinquish them if necessary, and to work instead for a more meaningful liturgical and parish communal life. (If, as most statistics indicate, it is the home atmosphere and the parental attitude toward religion which are the most decisive influences in shaping children's religious convictions, then why not concentrate on educating the parents to teach religion? Why wouldn't that, combined with a rich parish life, work as well as the present system? These are questions which a few are coming to ask.)

Few of these undercurrents, however, appear in the public debate on aid to religious schools. The stand of the bishops, in particular, in the national arena has been less nuanced. Their concern, traditionally enough, has been to preserve the existing school system. They have been vocally worried that a massive program of federal aid to the public schools alone would pose a major threat to religious schools. In addition, they believe that such a program would work an injustice on the religious schools and on Catholic parents; would be inconsistent with the non-discriminatory aid now given to the colleges under some federal programs; would ignore the contribution of the religious school to the good of the nation. Though the bishops themselves do not by any means have harmonious views on the issues—some favor federal aid, some do not— they have given the impression that they will oppose any federal aid bill which does not include aid to religious schools. (I use the word "impression" deliberately since it has been denied that any threats have ever been issued in this regard.)

Just how much actual financial danger a federal aid program would pose to the Catholic school system is, of course, conjectural. What is more certain is that a federal aid program which did not include religious schools would be one which ignored at least fifteen percent of American students and their potential contribution to the common good. At best, it would be dubious public policy to leave them out. More than that, their exclusion would further serve to increase the sense of discrimination felt by many Catholic parents that the following of their religious convictions imposes a heavy economic penalty. The complaint here is not that they are taxed to support the public schools (which they accept along with every other citizen), but that no tax assistance and few fringe-benefits are made available to them or to their schools despite the fact that these schools meet the normal state educational requirements. A large-scale federal aid program to public schools would heighten their sense of discrimination (normally supported by arguments from distributive justice). The bishops have seconded these complaints—and, on occasion, have helped to inspire them.

Even on the public level, however, there have been some important differences of opinion and emphasis among Catholics, both clerical and lay. Some bishops have pressed the point about the discriminatory implications of most recent federal aid bills far more aggressively than others. Their words have carried the strong suggestion of a threat. A few, whose opinions have been relatively unnoticed, have not supported that line of attack; they have avoided suggesting that Catholic support of federal aid to education should be dependent upon a share of aid for religious schools. On the whole, however, official agencies of the American Church—the N.C.W.C. most notably—have carried on a vigorous educational campaign among American Catholics, the aim of which is to impress upon them the justice of the "Catholic case" and to inform them of the situation and problems of the parochial schools.

My own position and that of my associates at *The Commonweal* has represented still another thread of opinion. We have opposed those who have argued dogmatically that the First Amendment necessarily excludes any kind of state aid to religious schools. On the contrary, we believe there is now a substantial body of constitutional lawyers who have shown many legitimate ways in which aid can be extended to religious schools. Moreover, we hold that the common good and sound public policy make some types of assistance feasible, legal and desirable. Other nations have solved the problem: Why can't we? At the same time, we have not felt that either our reading of the Constitution or those who see only an impregnable "wall of separation" can claim a monopoly of wisdom or a privileged insight. The courts have been ambiguous and vacillating over the years. But theirs is the final decision, and, since this is so, we have not joined the ranks of those Catholics who would institute a crusade shot through with righteous indignation. We share their concern, but can not and will not emulate their mood and tone.

Our main concern has been, instead, to attempt to keep the civil dialogue on the plane of rational discourse. This has meant a vigorous reaction against any hint (by any group within the American Church, high or low) that Catholics should exert political force to see their needs met. Given a choice, we would generally prefer that Catholics exercise the maximum amount of self-restraint.

That has not been our only concern. While we proclaim the importance of religious schools, both for religious reasons and for the good of pluralistic diversity in education, we have sometimes felt that Catholics do not accept the public schools with the enthusiasm necessary for meaningful support. However serious the problems of the religious schools, these problems are far less pressing than those that afflict, say, the urban public schools in slum neighborhoods. *De facto* segregation in hundreds of public schools, a dangerous drop-out rate among those minority groups which most need a complete education, underpaid teachers—all these critical difficulties in the public schools make the problems of Catholic schools seem comparatively tolerable. More than once have we wished that the N.C.W.C. would devote some of its energy to these public school matters; that the diocesan papers, which manage to find considerable space for the "Catholic case," would dramatize the plight of the public school; that bishops, pastors and lay organizations would put their minds to work on some of those American educational problems which do not directly concern Catholics. These are wishes which stem from a steady belief that Catholics should concern themselves with the common good; and, in education, that includes public schools every bit as much as religious schools.

In the past few years, for a variety of reasons, non-Catholics have shown themselves more sensitive to Catholic charges of injustice. Even if some hoary stereotypes about the Catholic schools manage to persist, they are less and less heard on the lips of non-Catholic leaders and thinkers. So, too, a growing Protestant and Jewish concern for religious education has helped develop a new sympathy for Catholic parents who desire to see their children instilled with religious convictions. The election of the late President Kennedy, improved Catholic–non-Catholic rapport, a renewed interest in all forms of education—all of these things have helped bring about a fresher climate of opinion.

What this suggests is that Catholics ought now to feel some measure of confidence that, in the years ahead, their legitimate needs will be recognized. The process may be slow and halting—but everything points in the direction of a resolution of some old dilemmas. More and more non-Catholics have spoken in favor of a fair share of aid to religious schools. More and more non-Catholics are urging the public (and Congress) to accept the very real contribution of religious schools to the national good. More and more non-Catholics see the anomaly in federal aid programs which include religious colleges but which exclude primary and secondary schools.

Why, in light of this highly visible trend, cannot Catholics now listen with equal sympathy to those who need their support to make public education what it should be? That is a question which Catholics should be asking themselves. For the non-Catholic, he might well ask himself whether, granting the constitutional difficulties, he has not sometimes used the Constitution as a handy smoke screen to conceal his worries about Catholic power and the ideals of a Catholic education.

The briar patch lies before us. As the essays which follow will suggest, there are many potential ways through it; and just as many potential blind alleys. Every way must be explored; every viewpoint must be considered. Above all, let the explorer keep one thing in mind: The way to get through a briar patch is by wriggling, squirming, twisting and keeping one's eyes open; and by listening to what one's companions have to say about the route. Try it any other way and you will get only scratches and wounds which fester.

GEORGE N. SHUSTER

Religion and Education

The question to be considered here is a complex and difficult one: If a young person is to be educated for our time
and our society, ought the study of religion to form part of
the training he receives? Note that we are not asking
whether he should learn about prayer and moral conduct
at home, go to church, and be taught the catechism or its
equivalent. Our question is also not whether he will listen
to sermons or read the Bible. All this will be taken for
granted, because our basic assumption here is that within
the framework of American society some form of Christian
or Jewish commitment can be postulated. For it would be
futile to inquire whether those who are anti-religious
should insist that their children be educated in religion.
But we may doubtless add that the commitment of which
we speak will in all probability suggest (later on in the
young life) some interest in and concern with other great
religions such as Buddhism and Islam. In the world of the
present these creeds are both sources of conflict and of a
sense of spiritual community, of profound divergence as
well as of comradeship.

To us of the present, education means bringing huge
groups of human beings, young and adult, into association
with bevies of teachers, more or less neatly arranged in
tiers, who are supposed to help the learning process along.

The term "supposed" is as old as pedagogical theory. Some observers, from Socrates to Robert Hutchins, have taken a very dim view of what most of their colleagues were doing. And in a different context, akin to what we are stressing here, Gordon Chalmers said: "It is altogether possible that despite the fanfare of post-war reform the American education system will continue to promote moral adolescence." It is desirable to bear these strictures in mind because otherwise we might be bowled over by the magnificence of the educational structure we have created. It is the biggest, most lavishly supported, most engrossingly complex in the world. But that is no guarantee that it happens to be worth very much. I myself believe it is pretty good—far from perfect, sometimes rheumatic, always exposed (even as religion in the broadest sense is) to the best and the worst in human nature.

Who in this vast conglomeration of classrooms is to teach religion? What is he to teach? And why? We can answer only in the context of our society and our system of education. The British decision after 1945 to grant State support to religious schools was based on what seemed at the time a vital need to build up the moral strength of the nation. How to avoid tumbling into so ghastly a trap as Nazism was one problem, and how to muster strength to fend off attack from it if it was tumbled into abroad was another.

In the United States we did not go this far, but something roughly comparable was undertaken. This was to foster through the schools an awareness of the agreement which it was believed had been reached concerning the purposes of our society. It was deemed a free society, the citizens of which had concurred through covenant, law and well-established tradition that the religious conscience is to be protected against constraint by government. Moreover, all Americans, regardless of their racial or national origins, are to be supported in their right not merely to equal treatment under the law but also to a just share of the benefits which accrue from a proper ordering of institutions. They shall not be discriminated against in education, economic opportunity and that measure of social status which is the product of community effort. Finally, every citizen can be expected to abide by whatever laws are just and subscribed to by the majority because only so can the dignity and maturity of the social order be preserved. However signally the American people may have succeeded or failed in making this agreement a social reality, there can be no doubt that public and private education joined with zest in making this ethic a fundamental concern of school life and study.

Almost automatically, the adoption of such a program greatly intensified the people's interest in religion. The "values" emphasized had their roots in religious faith, however valiantly some social philosophers might try to discover a few elsewhere. Therefore it was not surprising that a desire for schools conducted under religious auspices should increase not only among Catholics but among Jews and Protestants as well. But it was perhaps more significant that the public schools also responded, though the impact of religion upon them varied considerably from region to region.

Whereas a century earlier Catholics and Protestants had wrangled over proselytizing and therefore banned religious teaching from most of the public schools, there now seemed to have come about a quiet conspiracy between them—a conspiracy in which Jewish teachers often joined—to smuggle in as much of it as possible. Released-time (as well as the more traditional Sunday School) became a national institution, legally sanctioned; and youngsters who took advantage of it were likely to find that teachers they knew in school also taught the classes in religion. A network of observances, from Christmas assemblies to Seders, were introduced. And although no formal instruction was permitted, classes in art, music, history, and literature strongly stressed religious motifs. Indeed, until the ill-starred Regents' prayer was introduced and banned by the Supreme Court, the public schools in many areas of the United States probably paid more attention to religion than did similar schools in Great Britain.

I do not know what effect the recent decisions of the Supreme Court will have on all this, but it is probably safe to say that the formal expressions of religious interest are outlawed. At the present time, the principal of a high school could greet an assembly of students with excerpts from *Lady Chatterley's Lover,* but he must respect the tabu on reading from the Psalmist. Quite apart from the law, this is ridiculous. In all probability the Court, once it decided to hear the argument, could have arrived at no other verdict. But why it did not leave the regulation of education to the several states, which have traditionally exercised it, is a query which cannot easily be answered. Nevertheless I feel that public school educators, very many of whom are devout Christians and Jews, will not be so easily overawed by the Court. Mr. Justice Jackson in his day surmised that nobody could instruct in the Reformation without offending one creed or other. The fact of the matter is that this problem had long since been solved. And one can probably predict that since it is quite impossible to treat of any aspect of cultural, social or political history without reference to religion, the public schools will merely change the points of emphasis. Even so it is true that they have been dealt a rude and heavy blow.

Meanwhile the schools conducted under religious auspices have tried hard to determine what the role of the
teacher of religion is. We cannot join here in the current
debate about methodology, even if the writer were competent to do so (which he is not). In so far as formal
instruction in the creed is concerned, the focus of the discussion has not changed greatly since the days of Newman's
differences with Cardinal Cullen. On the one side are
those who feel that the schools should resemble seminaries
and novitiates as closely as possible. On the other one finds
those who, like the great Cardinal, would assure to
theology a central position in an area of science and literature which is largely autonomous. If we now transfer our
attention to the pattern of social behavior about which a
large measure of agreement was reached, the central question becomes: how valid, how firm, how deep is the
religious commitment in this hour?

To what extent does the faith of Christians and Jews
stand ready to quicken the American conscience in terms
of personal integrity and social justice? How often does
the corporate stance it assumes reflect the quality of mercy
and compassion? It is as obvious as anything can well be
that these questions must be directed in the first instance
to the religious teacher. If the instruction he gives is designed to elicit an affirmative response, and if it actually
does so, all Americans can be grateful. But if neither the
first nor the second hypothesis proves valid, the religious
mission is to some extent at least a failure. This is as true
of the professedly religious school as it is of other forms
of religious instruction.

On the other hand the religious commitment is, by its
very nature, something radically set apart from every form
of consensus about our society. It demands allegiance to

its own order of being, which is life within the Covenant God has made with man. It accepts, humbly and with no thought of profit in the temporal order, that which it believes has been revealed of the Divine Reality. The religious outlook is always profoundly eschatological. Knowing that not only does each human life end in dust, at best remembrance, but also that earth itself will pass, leaving no trace of Dante or the Parthenon, of electronics or nuclear fission, it chooses to believe in a Transcendent Goodness which in divers ways has made Itself known. This creed, which repudiates all forms of nihilism, is its own proper manifesto. Were the United States to be destroyed and all its institutions cease to exist, the Jewish and Christian faiths would remain inviolate in whatever ghettos elsewhere might house those who subscribed to them. This, then, must also be the message of Christian education, however dark the glass in which it sees Divinity or however discordant the many voices which proclaim the vision may seem to be.

What follows is that the teaching of religion must seek to reveal and infuse into the human spirit a life-changing awareness of *both* the social ethic which is derived from man's dignity and the reverence which is the prelude to the worship of God. Those who are the teachers must work in the profound conviction that what they are doing is more important than everything else; and so their formation is the heart of the matter. It will not suffice to cram into them compendia of doctrine, however carefully formulated by competent theologians and historians. They must likewise have a sixth sense for the pertinence of belief and practice to our time and the people who live in it. Paraphrasing Tertullian, they will believe it at once absurd that they should be spokesmen for the things of God and ridiculous that every man should not be such a spokesman. They will return again and again to empty places—hearts in which God speaks no more, families in which the pledge has been broken, the market place where the idols wear new faces but are very old.

It is implicit in what has been said that in principle nobody can tell whether the teaching of religion is more effective in professedly religious schools than it is outside them. The reason is that we simply do not know where the great, gifted, charismatic teachers are. Neither Bishop Sheen nor Billy Graham is teaching in a parochial or private school. It may be that the Sister who teaches mathematics well is rooting youngsters in their faith more securely than some one who teaches Scripture badly. Perhaps we shall in due time have dependable empirical evidence to help out here. For the moment we do not have any, and so we should doubtless be modest in making claims. At least I have found out recently that teaching Brothers and Sisters are quite restrained about this and other matters of importance.

Though what has been said remains true on all levels of education, the university adds a new dimension. This is: the university proper is intrinsically devoted not to the dispensing of information about human and cosmic reality but to its exploration. Its function is the constant revision of what is known, because this revision is the sole guarantee we have that the limited human intelligence can come even remotely near comprehending not all (this will forever be impossible) but some part of reality. We can dimly apprehend what this process means if we reflect on what happened after the revision of Newtonian physics by quantum physics. It follows that the scope allotted to religion in the university must be consonant with university purpose, or in other words that the study of theology must enter the realm of free inquiry, of the revision of what is known.

This may at first sight seem an unwarranted demand, but it is not, even though the basic difficulties of clarification are very great. Let us try to see what is involved. First, there can be no question of the revision, or whittling down, or "modernizing" of dogmatic teaching. The truths given to us through Revelation are, to paraphrase the language of the popes, beyond time, are eternal; and therefore revision of them is as impossible as it is to change the fact that we are human beings living on a planet in the solar system. But the "deposit of the Faith" is given to men who are in time; and therefore what they think about it, say about it, will reflect the age in which they have lived, the quality of their education, the power of the images they use. It is a sobering fact that for decades the early Church had no written accounts of Christ's life upon the earth, and that until St. Jerome's time no one had made a determined effort to see which of the accounts then being circulated were authentic. Therefore every form of textual literalism in the interpretation of Scripture was quite impossible in the early Church. How fortunate the nineteenth century would have been if it too had been emancipated from the a-b-c-ism which made such controversies as that about evolution lamentably violent and unnecessary.

Certainly it would not be possible to give the theological discipline status in the university unless at the very least it kept abreast of historical scholarship in the sense that it took careful stock of the changes in the meaning of words and concepts which always mark the shift from culture to culture, from generation to generation. Nor can this scholarship dispense with great latitude in the exercise of judgment. For instance, the notable modern interpretive histories of the Reformation, as written by such Catholic scholars as Grisar and Lortz, are profoundly different from each other. They have to be because every science must proceed from the conception of ideas about the problem to be explored to as much verification of those ideas as the evidence will permit. I think this is now pretty much taken for granted in the Church, but there are other things which as yet are not established and which as a result make it seem doubtful to many that the study of theology, in the Catholic sense, can proceed in harmony with the general spirit of the contemporary university.

These things for the most part are encountered in the study of man and his environment. That a scholar can go from general principles about the human psyche to an analysis of what conduct and conscience are and ought to be, without taking into account the results of modern analysis of psychic states is, for example, exceedingly dubious to many. Still it is a tenable thesis, provided that within the university context no one contends that it is more than that—is, for example, a "Catholic way" of dealing with psychology in its heights and depths. Thus the sexual urge is, as St. Paul recognized, a most powerful one, which marriage can to some extent channel and curb. But if Freud and his colleagues have done nothing else they have shown that the driving force of sex is so powerful because it is rooted in experience over which none of us could have exercised conscious control. A moral philosophy which does not reckon with this and other insights must therefore seem, in the university, a limited enterprise and one which has cut itself adrift from the thought of the time.

It is not going to be easy to resolve a problem such as

this, which is not at all the product of incompatibility but of a difference—a time lag—in the development of theologians. The university has gone its modern revolutionary way while theology for the most part was moving far less rapidly. One supposes that the effort to be made now does not assume that the gap can be closed at once or even soon. Rather what we can fruitfully do is to observe the steps taken by significant contemporary theologians—most of them Europeans, though some are, thank God, of our country and time—to move nearer to a solution of the problem. What is so remarkable about these men is that they have reconciled in their persons orthodoxy and freedom of inquiry. They have demonstrated once more that it is far harder to conjure up heterodoxy in the university than outside it. The reason is rather simple. A scholar does not suppose that a hypothesis he tests is a new revelation, as did Mohammed and Brigham Young. It is nothing more than a guess, an idea, which of its very nature must be examined and re-examined, and which in the end may be superseded. The good scholar is always trained to realize the limitations of the human mind, even when he recognizes them in others more clearly than in himself.

It seems to me that when theology has found its place in the university the art of teaching it will be accepted fully and generously by students and the professors of other disciplines. For then it will not simply be doing over again, with perhaps greater subtlety and more footnotes, what is appropriately done in the secondary school and which, because repetition is ingrained in it, fosters a not too glamorous boredom. Only we must always remember that religion is never only learning about religion. It is the quest for sanctity, the yearning for the voice of God in the room where one has sat quietly for twenty-four hours, the awe and the surrender of worship. For my part I think it is the Liturgy, therefore, which in the end binds all the forms and levels of Catholic religious teaching (and in other senses, Protestant and Jewish teaching) into a sacred unity. For it never forgets the divine treasure so lavishly expended, nor does it assume that ignorance is orthodoxy. It is the human community, wise and foolish, sinning and redeemed, young and old, welcoming one another into the company of God, Father, Son and Holy Spirit.

A Changing Pattern

Historically, since the American Catholic youngster was not made to feel at home in the public school, wherever possible he went to his own school. After 1840, when attempts to gain public support for New York parochial schools failed, Catholic interest and energy began to be expended almost exclusively on Catholic parochial and private schools, leaving the public schools as a semi-Protestant domain. In the decade following the Civil War, popular education began to take hold everywhere. In 1880 public school enrollment reached one million; by 1900 it had soared to 15 million and by 1920 to 21 million. Under the impetus of the school legislation passed in 1884 by the Third Plenary Council of Baltimore, Catholic school enrollment also began to mount. At the turn of the century, there were 854,523 pupils in Catholic schools and by 1920 this number had more than doubled to 1.8 million. The current enrollment in Catholic schools is 5.5 million or 14 percent of the nation's total elementary and secondary school population. But this achievement has not been without a price—in more than dollars. Thoughtful leaders within the Church are calling for a reappraisal of certain traditional practices and policies, for American Catholics also confront a period of decision.

Since the Third Council of Baltimore, an ideal of Catholic education has been held up: "Every Catholic child in a Catholic school." After eighty years of almost superhuman exertion to realize this ideal, it remains as distant as always. Better than five million of today's Catholic youngsters—two-thirds of those of high school age and about 40 percent of those of elementary school age—are not enrolled in Catholic schools. Within the current framework of operation, these children are not going to get even a partial Catholic schooling. In fact, the number of the unaccommodated will be greater each succeeding year.

In July of 1963, the chairman of the school board of the Archdiocese of Cincinnati, Auxiliary Bishop Paul F. Leibold, announced that, because the archdiocese faced a financial crisis, it would probably be necessary to drop the first four grades from Cincinnati Catholic schools. In any event, no further school construction was to be undertaken until there were an adequate supply of trained teachers and funds to properly compensate them. A few weeks earlier the Rochester Diocese had announced that after September there would be a ban on new Catholic schools and on expansion of existing schools for the immediate future. A year earlier, the Cardinal-Archbishop of St. Louis had laid down a similar policy for his archdiocese. The bishops of Saginaw, Spokane, Kansas City, Fargo, Richmond and Green Bay have all been forced to adjust to the shortage of teachers and classrooms by curtailing one or more of the grades in their schools.

What has happened? Have the archbishops and bishops of these dioceses abandoned the ideal of Catholic education? Has the drive for Catholic schools finally run out of steam? Not at all. To begin with, the demand by parents for Catholic education for their youngsters has not slackened in the least. A spot check taken of eight diocesan school systems in the summer of 1963 revealed that principals had been forced to turn away some 37,000 applicants —19,000 for elementary and 18,000 for secondary grades.

With some exceptions the quality of Catholic elementary and secondary schooling, like that of the public schools—and for much the same reasons—is steadily improving. The total enrollment year after year continues to rise. No; Catholic leadership in the United States is not doing an about-face, but is at last facing up to some of the hard realities of the present and the inviting challenges of the future. Despite the impressive accomplishments of the Catholic schools over the past eighty years—and they are truly many—Catholic leadership is beginning to realize that some of the successful patterns of the past have served their purpose. New approaches, new emphases, new methods are called for to continue achieving the perennial goals of Catholic education.

It is taking nothing from the leadership of the past—from the men of courage and vision who were the architects of today's monument—to enumerate four less-than-beneficient outcomes of the drive since 1884 for universal Catholic education in this country. They are: 1) clerical domination of the schools; 2) over-commitment to the elementary school; 3) confusion of the academic mandate and the pastoral charge; 4) substitution of the school for the family and Church as the primary agent in the religious formation of the child.

Of necessity, from earliest times, the conduct of Catholic education in America has been the almost exclusive charge of the clergy and the religious orders. There was little alternative and large precedent for this policy. From the financial point of view there simply would not have been money for even the modest salaries that teachers generally receive. Moreover, there is a rich tradition of clerical and religious activity in education. In many European countries the schools of the religious teaching groups, such as the Brothers of the Christian Schools and the Jesuits have always been held in the highest regard. A convent-school education for girls had always been considered by affluent Catholics (and often non-Catholics) as conferring a special cachet. Consequently, congregations of teaching nuns and Brothers were invited over from Europe. Dozens of native American congregations of sisters were founded. The contributed services of these dedicated men and women made it possible to open schools on an undreamed of scale.

Until 1945 there seemed to be a steady, though always insufficient, supply of vocations, especially to the sisterhoods, but since then the demand has galloped wildly ahead of the supply. In addition, the standards of teacher preparation for all schools have been considerably elevated so that it takes longer to train a teaching nun. At one time there may have been basis for the criticism that many women religious teachers began their classroom careers without the equivalent collegiate and professional training of their public-school counterparts. It was true that many congregations of sisters had the practice of putting teachers to work with only two years of concentrated preparation. These young teachers would then take additional professional courses in a series of summer schools, eventually completing work for a college degree.

There was always some warrant for this practice, which, until a few decades ago, was not uncommon among teachers going into public schools. The fact that the young sister lived in a convent community of veteran teachers and was able to profit from close, friendly supervision and counseling could be viewed as more than adequate compensation for any delay in taking extra courses in formal pedagogy.

The establishment in 1953 of the National Sister Formation Conference, however, has worked a quiet revolution among the women's congregations. The idea of the conference is, as one leader has stated it, "that sisters doing active works in our own times need a long and careful spiritual formation, a general intellectual training which will equip them for a rich personal life and an effective social leadership, and a precise professional preparation which will make them the equals or superiors of lay people doing the same kind of work." That this far-seeing policy is being successfully implemented is attested to by the temporary halt to school expansion in many dioceses. The mainstay of the Catholic elementary and secondary school remains the teaching nun. In 1961, some 100,000 sisters were in the classroom. Nearly 50,000 lay teachers, an average of between three and four for every one of the 13,000 Catholic schools, are teaching alongside them. But most remarkable of all, the percentage of lay teachers in elementary schools has leaped from 7.1 in 1950 to 29.5 in 1961, and on the secondary school level from 16.6 in 1950 to 26.7 in 1961.

Though the lay teacher in numbers arrived late, he is here to stay—to the great strengthening of the Catholic system. Obviously school population pressures had most to do with altering the old pattern, but new attitudes in the Catholic community would have brought the change about regardless. In planning any future expansion in Catholic education, the key figure will be the lay teacher. Qualified religious teachers will of course continue to shoulder much of the burden, but also making their own rich contribution to the academic ideals and religious tone of the school will be the lay teacher. And finally, it might be pointed out that the increased lay presence in the parochial school will mean a lessening of the mistrust the strong sectarian nature of these institutions once inspired in the community.

When in 1884 the Third Plenary Council of Baltimore ordered that a school was to be established near every church "within two years," the school envisaged was an elementary school—the type of school which circumscribed the needs and ambitions of the overwhelming majority of Americans of that era. Eighty years later Catholic emphasis still remains on the elementary school despite the enormous changes in the schooling pattern of American society.

It is patent that the high school has replaced the elementary school as the center of loyalties and educational influences for the American citizen. Moreover, even this is changing. Increasingly the thirteenth and fourteenth years, the junior college, are becoming a normal part of the educational pattern.

The theory can be fairly argued, whether the earlier or later years are psychologically more important in the child's formation. But there is no argument over the fact that today the secondary school and/or the college play a much more dominant role in the life of a young person. The child's recreation, hobbies, and amusements; his physical weakness, affections and sense of dependence naturally keep him closer to his home and family. During these delicate years the school obviously is important in helping to mould character but its influence is less than the family's.

On the contrary, once a boy or girl begins high school, from the distribution of his or her waking hours alone, it is clear that the school has the ascendancy in influence. Now not only are classes and studies and friendships centered at school but the ever increasing whirl of co-curricular and extra-curricular activities engages the high school student six days and more of each week. Thirty years ago, the platform orator could nostalgically refer to his happy childhood at P.S. 64 or Evergreen Grammar School. Today identification is never with the elementary school but with the high school or the college.

Current shortages of classrooms and teachers have forced Catholic leaders to face this problem squarely. Archbishop Lawrence J. Shehan of Baltimore, when president-general of the National Catholic Educational Association, said in a keynote address to the national convention:

"In certain localities where with existing plant, personnel and resources it seems impossible to provide full Catholic education for all Catholic children, the question has been raised about the advisability of offering to every child Catholic education at a certain level. Since young children are more completely under the control of their parents, since it is common experience that during the younger years attention and interest can be held by extra-curricular religious instruction, and since neither of these conditions holds true during the years of adolescence, thought might well be given to a plan to provide all children with Catholic education, say from the seventh to the twelfth grade. At least we would have nothing to lose and perhaps much to gain if carefully planned and observed experiments were tried in areas where the full course of Catholic education cannot be offered to all children at the present time."

The overcommitment of the Catholic Church in the United States to the elementary school has diverted money, personnel and attention from the secondary schools. Few dioceses can presently accommodate in their high schools the yearly graduating classes from the elementary schools. Back in 1900 about 10 percent of the total population of high school age was attending secondary schools, and three out of four high school graduates continued on to college. In 1961, 90.2 percent of high-school age youngsters was in high school, and more than half the graduating class went on to college. Many dioceses are unwilling or unable to make the adjustment called for by these drastic changes in the American school pattern with the result that most of their high-school-age youngsters are in public schools.

If the development of secondary school education has flagged because of preoccupation with elementary schools, what should be said of the plight of American Catholic colleges and universities? His verdict is of course less valid now than in 1941, but D. W. Brogan's candid appraisal, that "in no modern Western society is the intellectual prestige of Catholicism lower than in the country where, in such respects as wealth, numbers, and strength of organization, it is so powerful," could never have been made, if the colleges and universities had been supported by the Catholic community.

Since the building of elementary schools on such a scale drained the Catholic purse, there was not a great deal of money left for the support of higher education. With a handful of exceptions, the Catholic colleges and universities have received practically no financial support from the dioceses. As a consequence, even the six universities and twenty-five or so colleges which have achieved some stature in the academic community have not yet realized their full promise.

The third by-product of the heavy Catholic commitment to the elementary school has been gradually dissipating in recent years. This is the confusion of the academic mandate and the pastoral charge.

Some would explain the rationale of the Catholic school with the plain statement that it exists "to save souls." Though this is correct, it is seriously misleading. It would be just as true to say that the purpose of Catholic hospitals, youth clubs, summer camps and veterans organizations is "to save souls." The saving of souls is too general an explanation of the school's purpose and fails to indicate the specific objective or formal aspect, that which distinguishes the school as such from the hospital, the youth club, the summer camp and the veterans organization. Each of these activities has its own immediate and specifying end or purpose. Since the saving of souls is likewise the purpose of all these other works, it can be no more than a description of the school's ultimate purpose—a purpose the school necessarily shares in the absolute order with all human undertakings.

Could it not be objected, however, that in operating schools the Catholic Church is simply trying to make good Catholics, and the priests, brothers, sisters and even lay people who teach in them are agents of the Roman Catholic Church?

This objection is based on a confusion between the purpose of the work itself and the purpose or motive of the worker. Education is education, and a school is a school, regardless of the motives of those conducting it. In other words, the school guards its nature and basic purpose despite the reasons the Church or the State may have in sponsoring educational activity. The State enters into education because it wants its citizens to have an adequate knowledge of their civic duties and privileges, and to make sure they reach the level of physical, intellectual, and moral culture required for the common good. The Church establishes schools in order that these same persons as members of her communion will *better* acquire the supreme integrating principle of supernatural wisdom in ordering the knowledge, skills, and attitudes they acquire. Neither the motive of the State nor the motive of the Church essentially alters the nature of the school. The failure to make this distinction between the agent's motivation and the intrinsic formality of the work itself can lead to two different attitudes—both, in the final analysis, irrational.

In the one case, the result is the contrived dilemma wherein one is confronted with the stark choice of the flag or the cross, Fatherland or Faith, Caesar or God. This is the basis of the secularist demand put to Catholics at times that they choose between loyalty to a public school dedicated to producing Americans and the parochial school dedicated to producing Catholics. The Christian philosophy of education finds no real antagonism between the two ideals of dedicated citizenry and religious allegiance. They are compatible, one complementing the other.

In the other case, the saving of souls becomes for a minority of well-intentioned people the justification for academic practices and policies that fall far short of what is esteemed solid and scholarly in the education world. Happily, this criticism cannot be made of the overwhelming majority of the school systems, but it takes only a few egregious examples to provide ammunition for hostile critics of Catholic education. Especially is this true on the collegiate level.

Perhaps it is an unintentional compliment, for the same strictures are rarely passed with reference to the dozens of second-rate municipal, state or sectarian colleges springing up everywhere. Nonetheless, the proliferation of Catholic colleges, especially for women, has been the bewilderment of the academic community. Without endowment, without adequately trained faculty, without laboratory facilities and library holdings, without clear academic goals, a number of these institutions have bravely sprung up during the past thirty years, inspired by some vague apostolic mandate. The sponsoring group, as often as not, has enjoyed some success in high school work, and so feels thoroughly adequate to undertake college work. Sometimes the need to finance the teacher preparation and degree work of their own nuns by opening the doors of the projected college to a few hundred coeds has been an added incentive for religious or diocesan superiors, over and above the apostolic motive. In any event, for the most part they condemn themselves to the limbo of mediocrity, and in the academic marketplace they debase the general coinage of Catholic higher education.

The fourth and perhaps the most serious drawback resulting from the commitment to the elementary school made at the Council of Baltimore is the complete reversal of the roles of school and family-Church in the education of the child. This modern phenomenon is a growing source of concern to many bishops and pastors. Too many Catholic families feel absolved of any responsibility for the religious formation of their children once they have entrusted them to the parochial school. "Let the good sisters take care of it," is not an uncommon attitude. The result has been that on reaching school age, these youngsters are almost totally ignorant of their Catholic faith. In many Catholic homes there is no concerted effort by father or mother to supplement or complement the work of the school. This situation is far from the ideal of the family and school collaborating in the religious upbringing of the child.

But bad as this situation is, what of the homes of those five million Catholic children for whom there are no Catholic schools? In many instances the parish church is expected to undertake whatever training the boy or girl receives. Here and there, the education program of the Confraternity of Christian Doctrine is doing a thorough job, but hampered by a lack of funds and personnel (the money and teachers are all for the parochial school) the results must fall far short of the promise.

Meantime, a probable 75 percent of the time and energy of the pastor and his assistant is spent in fund-raising devices to keep the parish school afloat. Little time and energy, to say nothing of imagination and initiative, are left over to cope with the dual problem: how to train parents to do their job, how to build an effective religious education program to care for the hundreds of Catholic children in the public schools. In far too many parishes the school plant dwarfs the church, and school activities seem to completely dominate parish life. What is here forgotten is that the center of the parish must always be the liturgical life of its people.

This decade is putting new stresses and strains on both the public school and the Catholic school. These are obviously years of adjustment, both for Catholic education and for public school education. Some of these adjustments will be easier if they are made together. A chapter in the history of American education is closing. Beyond any doubt, striking changes will take place within both school systems and in their relations with one another in the years ahead.

Is it too much to expect that the recent years of what can even at times be called "sunny" dialogue between Protestants and Catholics are preparing for the day when cooperative ventures, like the shared-time Program or a completely overhauled released-time Program, will become part of public education? If in the past, the question of religion in education has been an almost constant source of Church-State tension and inter-church friction, in the future it may well become a bridge.

VIRGIL C. BLUM

Freedom and Equality

The question of the constitutionality of federal aid for church-related education must be discussed in terms of the rights and liberties of parents and their children. The inviolate character of the individual, his freedom of thought and belief—these are the central issues of the federal-aid-to-education debate that grips our nation today.

The centrality of the individual in questions touching thought and belief was underscored by Justice Felix Frankfurter in the Douds case (1950). "The cardinal article of faith of our civilization is the inviolate character of the individual," he wrote. Hence, he continued, "a man can be regarded as an individual and not as a function of the state only if he is protected to the largest possible extent in his thoughts and in his beliefs as the citadel of his person."

Most of man's struggles throughout history have, in fact, been efforts to win for himself the freedom that is essential to his individuality. The quest for freedom of thought and belief has been universal and continuous. From the Athenians and early Christians, to the opponents of the Inquisition and Communism, the human spirit has cried out most incessantly for freedom of thought and belief. Man strives so constantly for this freedom because without it his rational nature is impeded in its most lofty activities —his search for finite and infinite truth.

This desire to be free in thought and belief, says Pope John in *Pacem in Terris,* is rooted in man's nature. "By the natural law," he declares, "every human being has the right . . . to freedom in search for truth and in expressing and communicating his opinions . . . [And] every human being has the right to honor God according to the dictates of an upright conscience. . ."

This intense natural yearning to be free in thought and belief explains why parents, wherever they are denied full and real freedom in the education of their children, are restless and discontent until this freedom is won. And, significantly, wherever this fundamental freedom has been won, a high degree of religious peace, harmony and co-operation marks the relations between the different religions. This, the present writer found to be the case in Holland, Germany, Denmark, in Belgium, England, Scotland and Ireland.

The importance to America of a real parental choice in education, of freedom in the pursuit of truth, was emphasized by the Supreme Court almost forty years ago in the Pierce case (1925): "The fundamental theory of liberty upon which all governments in this Union repose excludes any general power of the state to standardize its children by forcing them to accept instruction from public teachers only." To this writer, therefore, the central issue in the federal-aid-to-education debate is freedom of thought and freedom of belief in the pursuit of truth. To debate the issue in terms of schools, impregnable walls, and churches, is like debating freedom of speech in terms of lecture halls, TV towers, and synagogues. These matters may or may not be relevant, but they are at best secondary or incidental.

Constitutional rights, in other words, are personal. The right to be free in thought and belief, and to share equally in federal aid to education is a personal right; it does **not** inhere in schools, churches or synagogues. Here, as in the segregation cases, it is the individual child who is entitled to be treated equally before the law.

In this context, a closer look at the constitutional question may be profitable. The state has a vital interest in the education of children. And, although the several states subsidized the teaching of Protestantism in our public schools for the greater part of a century, today the state is primarily, if not exclusively, interested in the education of children in secular subjects, which deal only with things of *this* world.

Moreover, it is because of the state's proper interest in the secular education of children that the Supreme Court has on several occasions pointed out that the education of children in secular subjects in church-related schools serves a public purpose. "It is much too late," said the Court in the Everson bus-ride case (1947), "to argue that legislation intended to facilitate the opportunity of [church-related school] children to get a secular education serves no public purpose."

The education of children in reading, 'riting, and 'rithmetic serves a public purpose. And this public purpose is achieved whether the subjects are taught by a Jewish rabbi, a Lutheran minister, or a Catholic nun. Nor is the secular character of these and other secular subjects changed when taught in a Jewish, Lutheran, or Catholic school. Further, a religious permeation of secular subjects does not change their essentially secular character.

On the other hand, neutrality in the classroom is impossible. This is true of the physical and life sciences, but it is particularly true of the humanities and the social sciences. There is hardly a subject taught that does not directly or indirectly give rise to the fundamental questions of life. Is there a God? Was Christ divine? What is the nature of man? Right or wrong—with reference to what? The freedom and equality of man—why? Justice or injustice—with reference to what norm? What is man's moral responsibility, if any? These questions are religious, or basically so. And the intelligent teacher in interpreting his subject matter cannot avoid them. Consciously or subconsciously, he inculcates either his own religious values or the religious value commitment of his school.

The answers which teachers give to these and other questions establish the religious values of their classrooms and of their school. These values may be Protestant, Catholic, Jewish or secularist.

I do not use the term secularism in a pejorative sense. Protestant theologian Robert McAfee Brown says "Secularism is itself a faith; it is a religion." The Supreme Court agrees with him. So do I. The faith of the secularist is totally in himself and in the things of this world. For him, God, if there is a God, is wholly irrelevant to the daily business of life, and indeed to all human affairs. Man is sufficient unto himself. Secularism, Harvard President Nathan Pusey says, "has itself become a *faith* and raised a hope than man can through his own efforts—without God— solve all the remaining problems which stand between him and a secular paradise on earth."

A school with a secularist orientation has an unmistakable religious impact on children. Using the term "religion" in its traditional sense, Dr. Luther A. Weigle, former dean of the Yale Divinity School, says: "The ignoring of religion by the schools inevitably conveys to the children a negative suggestion . . . it is natural for them to conclude that religion is negligible, or unimportant, or irrelevant to the main business of life." And the English educator Sir Walter Moberly, in denying the possibility of neutrality in the classroom, maintains that when you omit God from the classroom you "insinuate silently, insidiously, and all but irresistibly" that he "is a matter of secondary importance."

In every school, therefore, secular subjects are taught, and, moreover, a religious orientation is given to these subjects. In church-related schools, in addition to the secular subjects and their religious orientation, sacred or religious subjects are taught. It is important to repeat at this point that the essentially secular character of a secular subject is not changed by the religious orientation or permeation it receives in a Protestant, Catholic, Jewish or secularist school.

Whenever government supports the education of children in secular subjects, it aids one or more religions. Religious values, to a greater or lesser degree, permeate all teaching. Such aid to religion is not direct; it is incidental. It is the by-product of legislation enacted for a secular purpose—the education of children in secular subjects. It is not aid to religion *as* religion; therefore, there can be no question as to its constitutionality.

At this point, however, it will be profitable to consider in more detail the exact nature of the aid that accrues to religion when government aids children in church-related schools, and the constitutional question raised. Thereafter, I shall bring the issue to focus on the question of freedom of thought and belief in education.

Dr. Robert M. Hutchins sees no constitutional difficulty in federal aid for the education of church-related school children in secular subjects. The fact that such education "is 'permeated' by religion," or that federal aid for such education is an "aid to religion," he says, "is immaterial." The benefit that accrues to religion, Hutchins argues, is "incidental to an overriding public benefit." Consequently, "such incidental benefits," he reasons, "do not invalidate the legislation."

Dr. Hutchins is here following the "common-sense" doctrine enunciated by the Supreme Court in the Zorach released-time case of 1954. Speaking of "the constitutional standard" of separation of Church and State, Justice William O. Douglas said: "The problem, like many problems in constitutional law, is one of degree." This is the rejection of a rigid absolutism in favor of a flexible relativity. The Court there, moreover, emphasized this rejection of absolutism in Church-State relations when it declared: "The First Amendment does not say that in every and all respects there shall be a separation of Church and State." The government can, within the limits of this doctrine, enact legislation for a secular purpose even though the legislation incidentally benefits religion.

The Court adhered to this doctrine in the Sunday closing law cases of 1961. It held that closing laws enacted for a "secular purpose"—rest, repose, relaxation, and family visiting—are not invalid because they incidentally benefit the Christian religions. In other words, the sovereign power of government to legislate for the general welfare, or for the national defense, is not stifled when such legislation results in incidental benefits to religion. That is, the no-aid principle does not limit or render impotent the power of the federal and state governments to legislate for those secular purposes for which they were established.

This doctrine was also articulated by the Maryland Court of Appeals in the Wheat bus-ride case (1938) when it declared: "The fact that the private schools, including parochial schools, receive a benefit from it could not prevent the Legislature's performing the public function." The reason for this, said the court, is that "the institution must be considered as aided only *incidentally,* the aid only a *by-product* of proper legislative action" (emphasis added).

Chief Justice Charles E. Hughes, however, gave this doctrine its most authoritative expression for a unanimous Court in the Cochran case (1930) in which the Court upheld a Louisiana textbook law. The law was attacked as violating the establishment clause of the First Amendment since it provided textbooks for church-related school children. The Court rejected the contention. Hughes reasoned: "The legislation does not segregate private schools, or their pupils, as its beneficiaries or attempt to interfere with any matters of exclusively private concern. *Its interest is education broadly; its method, comprehensive. Individual interests are aided only as the common interest is safeguarded*" (emphasis added).

The intent of the legislature was to achieve a public purpose, to promote the common interest; benefits which accrue to individual interests are incidental. The Court, moreover, considered the argument that a degree of religious instruction permeated the church-related school curriculum, *and unanimously rejected this argument as an irrelevant consideration.* The reason for this is clear. Said the Court: "We can not doubt that the taxing power of the State is exerted for a *public purpose*" (emphasis added).

In other words, when the government enacts legislation for a public purpose, incidental benefits which may accrue to a religion are irrelevant to the question of its constitutionality. Such incidental benefits to religion can not paralyze the federal and state governments for those actions that are deemed necessary for the welfare of the people or for the national defense.

There is, therefore, compelling legal authority to sustain the conclusion that the federal government can validly subsidize the education of church-related school children in secular subjects. Against the principles of law enunciated by the Court in the Cochran and Everson cases, and reinforced eight to one in the Snyder bus-ride case of 1961, the opponents of freedom in education can come up with nothing more convincing than the Everson *obiter dictum* which forbids aid to religion. An *obiter dictum* is a side-pronouncement by the Court which, while deserving respectful attention, has absolutely no legal binding force.

It should be noted, moreover, that even as the Court pronounced the Everson no-aid-to-religion *dictum,* it rejected the argument than an incidental benefit to religious education nullifies the state's power to achieve a public purpose. It there upheld state-provided bus rides for church-related school children as a public function, despite the fact that such rides result in an incidental benefit to religion.

There can be no question, therefore, that, for example, federal tuition grants for the study of secular subjects in church-related schools are constitutional. Few people would maintain that such grants, provided as part of a general federal-aid program, serve no public purpose; and few, if judicial precedents are accepted, would contend that the incidental benefits which accrue to religion nullify the government's power to promote the general welfare and to provide for the national defense with a program of aid to education designed, through instruction in secular subjects, to develop the brainpower of every American child.

In the world of today, our national power is directly contingent upon our brainpower, our intellectual and technological excellence. The nation's brainpower must, therefore, be developed to its highest potential for the national security and in readiness for war. This our national government can do, apart from constitutional grants, under its power to wage war. This power is an attribute of sovereignty, and, when the government legislates to develop the nation's brainpower, it cannot be nullified by incidental benefits which, as a byproduct of the legislation, accrue to religion.

There is little debate about the constitutionality of federal aid for the education of church-related college students in secular subjects. The G.I. Bill of Rights, the War Orphans Educational Assistance Act, and a multiplicity of federal programs under which the government subsidizes tens of thousands of graduate and undergraduate students in church-related colleges make the debate academic. Yet, if federal aid is constitutional on the college level, its constitutionality on the elementary-secondary level is even more compelling. This is consequent upon the fact that elementary-secondary education is *compulsory,* while college education is optional. The Supreme Court made it unmistakably clear in the Barnette case (1943) that, for this reason, elementary and secondary school children are entitled to greater protection of freedom of conscience than college students.

This brings us back to the fundamental issue of the federal-aid-to-education debate: the question of freedom. The above arguments in support of the validity of federal aid for the study of secular subjects in church-related schools, although conclusive, do not, in my opinion, get to the heart of the matter. The heart of the matter is, as I said, freedom—freedom of thought and freedom of conscience. It is a question of the integrity of the individual child, under his parents, in his thoughts and beliefs. It is a question of the freedom of the child to pursue particular secular truths and to associate them freely with his own religious convictions. To deny education-tax funds to a child because he wishes to relate truths to Infinite Truth, is to penalize him for his religious beliefs. In the words of Justice Hugo Black, "freedom to think is inevitably abridged when beliefs are penalized by impositions of civil disabilities."

Freedom of thought and belief received a ringing re-affirmation by the Supreme Court in the Barnette flag-salute case. The case called into question the validity of a West Virginia law which imposed economic penalties—expulsion from tax-supported schools—upon children who refused to conform to a state-established orthodoxy, the flag salute and pledge. It declared: "If there is any fixed star in our constitutional constellation, it is that no official, high or petty, can prescribe what shall be orthodox in politics, nationalism, religion or other matters of opinion." To reject this principle of personal freedom and integrity is to undermine the very foundations of individual freedom in a free society. Individual freedom is a myth when, through conditioned educational subsidies, thoughts and beliefs are controlled by the state.

Since the teacher of secular subjects inculcates particular religious values, it is beyond question a serious violation of freedom of conscience to coerce a child to conform to such values. When a child is compelled to attend a public school through economic sanctions, he is, in effect, coerced to conform to the religious values of the public school. These values constitute the state-established orthodoxy. The critical question of freedom of conscience, it should be pointed out, is not changed one iota whether the religious orthodoxy of the public school is Protestant, Catholic, Jewish or secularist.

The problem of freedom of conscience is critical because dissenters have equal rights with those who subscribe to the current orthodoxy. If children are denied equal education-tax benefits because they cannot in conscience accept the religious values of the public schools, their freedom of conscience is violated; they are penalized for their religious beliefs. The parents of such children are placed by the government in an intolerable dilemma. They must either accept religious values in their children's education which violently clash with their own cherished beliefs, or lose all government support for their children's education in secular subjects.

The imposition of such a choice by government was recently condemned by the Supreme Court in the Sherbert case (1963). This case dealt with a denial by South Carolina of unemployment compensation benefits to a Mrs. Sherbert, a Seventh Day Adventist, because she would not work on Saturday, the Sabbath Day of her faith.

In a 7 to 2 decision, the Court held that the state ruling "forces her to choose between following the precepts of her religion and forfeiting benefits, on the one hand, and abandoning one of the precepts of her religion in order to accept work, on the other hand." When the government imposes a choice of this kind, it impairs religious freedom. "Governmental imposition of such a choice," said the Court, "puts the same kind of burden upon the free exercise of religion as would a fine imposed against appellant for her Saturday worship."

Government imposition of a choice between education tax benefits, on the one hand, and freedom of religion in education, on the other, puts the same kind of burden upon the exercise of religion in the choice of school as would a fine imposed upon parents who send their children to church-related schools.

Justice Robert Jackson once remarked that government "must let man's mind alone." When government demands the right to manipulate, shape and form the child's thoughts and beliefs as a condition for sharing in education-tax funds, it is *not* letting man's mind alone. This is state-intrusion into and violation of the sanctuary of the child's soul. This is the child's personal domain. Such a violation of the freedom and integrity of the child is, I contend, in conflict with our principles as a free society. "The priceless heritage of our society," said Justice Jackson in the Douds case, "is the unrestricted constitutional right of each member to think as he wills. Thought control is a copyright of totalitarianism, and we have no claim to it."

I suspect it is Dr. Hutchins' revulsion to any kind of thought control that caused him to say: "Aid to all educational institutions that meet federal standards would promote religious freedom as well as education . . . it is a violation of the [First] Amendment to apply pressure, direct or indirect, upon the conscience of any person." An education-aid program which requires attendance at public schools as a condition for sharing in tax funds applies pressure, all too frequently irresistible, upon the conscience of millions of children, who, though they cannot in conscience accept the religious values of the public schools, must nevertheless accept them.

A well-conceived government policy of freedom in education would not result in a fragmentation of our school system. To avert such an undesirable consequence of freedom, we can learn from methods adopted in European democracies. Some of these methods of control are: (1) less than full equality for independent school children in federal and state education-tax support (the freedoms may be limited to the extent required by the common good); (2) government-fixed minimum enrollment for independent schools and academic standards based on educational considerations; and (3) a forfeiture penalty equal to fifteen percent of school construction costs on schools whose enrollment falls below the fixed minimum.

In view of the growing popular interest in the education issue, there is every indication that freedom and equality in education is the inexorable wave of the future. In the past two years public opinion has shifted sharply in the direction of freedom of thought and belief in education. According to the Gallup poll, opinion favoring the inclusion of church-related education in a federal aid program rose from 36 to 49 percent of those polled, with 7 percent expressing no opinion.

Of equal significance is the fact that today many Protestant, Catholic and Jewish parents are working together in true ecumenical spirit to promote the cause of academic freedom in the pursuit of truth. They are deeply interested not only in the religious education of their children, but also in the preservation of freedom and diversity in our democratic society. They know full well that, as the Supreme Court warned in the Barnette case, "compulsory unification of opinion achieves only the uniformity of the graveyard."

O'NEIL C. D'AMOUR

The Catholic Case

From the earliest days, foreign commentators have noted the unique role played by education in the progress of what is often called "the American experiment." Indeed, both foreign and native observers have assumed that the success of the American experiment would have been jeopardized, if not doomed to failure, without the peculiar emphasis on education. In the United States, for the first time in recorded history, a major nation undertook to provide an education for all of its citizenry.

Certainly, it is a tribute to the vision and foresight of the founding fathers that they perceived the vital need for an educated citizenry in a free democracy. It must be conceded that it would be difficult to overstress the important role played by the American school in the realization of the American dream. However, only too often observers and commentators tend to overlook, or neglect, the complexity of the educational history of this nation and to portray that history in such an over-simplified manner that it lacks objectivity.

The usual end results of such an over-simplification of history are a blurring of developmental lines and an identification of the *American* school with the secular, state, or public school of today. This portrayal, which incidentally is most avidly promoted by propagandists of certain interest groups and adopted by many uncritical citizens, is a dangerous portrayal. It is dangerous in that, in presenting a distorted view of history and tradition, it establishes a false base upon which the education of tomorrow is to be built. While a nation must not remain static and must not live in the past, a nation that ignores its past and is unaware of the facts that brought it to greatness endangers its future. This is particularly true of education because in the education of its young a nation forms its future.

While it may seem far from the wording of recent decisions of the United States Supreme Court, an objective viewing of the history of American education would establish the fact that its founders never conceived of the public school as a secular school. Furthermore, these founders would never have tolerated the view that the establishment of the public school represented a renunciation by the Church of its traditional rights in education. Far from intending to bring about a secular school system, they sought to provide for the vital continuation of religion in the schools.

As one reads the story of public school origins, two major objectives would seem to have been determinant of the course of events. First of all, those who were destined to have the greatest influence, including Horace Mann, were aware of the need to eliminate the often violent sectarian controversies that were threatening the quality of education. The solution they arrived at was not one of eliminating religion from the schools; it was rather that of creating a system of schools that was broadly Protestant in its nature, a system designed to perpetuate the Protestant Christian principles deemed to be fundamental to the American way of life and of government. The resulting system was a Protestant parochial school system supported by tax funds.

The second early objectives were those of curtailing the influence of the rising Catholic population and of providing an antidote to "papist" poison. It is not at all difficult to find explicit statements by prominent educators to the effect that the public schools should be used to lead immigrant Catholic children away from the errors of Rome. It was in response to these objectives of public education that Catholic citizens undertook to establish what was to become the Catholic parochial school system. In its origins the Catholic parochial school system is to be seen as a fortress designed to protect the Faith and culture of a beleaguered minority against the onslaughts of a majority sincerely bent on destroying both. The subsequent history of these two school systems—one, Protestant parochial, the other, Catholic parochial—is significant for the obtaining of a balanced view of educational problems and patterns in the second half of the twentieth century.

For the Protestant parochial school system the years brought about radical change. Following the turn of the century, almost imperceptibly, Protestant churches began to lose control of the schools. Having sought to use the power of the state to resolve its internecine sectarian warfare and to contain or destroy the Roman enemy, Protestantism found the interplay of forces within the secular state to be overwhelming. With the mounting immigration and with the rising secular spirit of the scientific age, the essentially Protestant government moved inevitably toward religious neutrality. Education having been entrusted to the state, by inexorable law followed the state into neutrality and then to the embrace of humanist philosophy. It is a tragic fact that Protestant leadership, having made the mistake of placing the church's educational rights in the hands of the state, did not seek at any time to regain those rights. Rather, blinded by fear and dislike of Catholicism, the Protestant leadership not only accepted the total usurpation of the right to educate by the state but even sought to justify the usurpation.

The consequence of the historical process is that today public education, generally speaking, is a totally secular education, dominated by the secular philosophy of life. This statement is not to be regarded in an invidious sense. Given the entrusting of the right to educate into the hands of the state, the result was inevitable. In a pluralist society such as that of the United States, a school system deemed to be the agency of the state must of necessity be religiously neutral, and religious neutrality always opens the way to secular humanism. The final declaration of the end of the public school as a Protestant parochial school is to be found in the decision on prayer and Bible reading rendered recently by the Supreme Court.

As public education went through its slow evolution, concurrently the Catholic school system evolved. The Catholic school system truly is a remarkable social and economic phenomenon. Logically, it would have seemed impossible that the Catholic people of the late-nineteenth century and early twentieth century should have been able even to think of establishing and maintaining a school system. Catholics generally were poverty-stricken and lacking in the background and skills to occupy any but the lowest rungs of the socio-economic ladder. However, these people not only established a school system but managed to maintain and expand that system in a truly remarkable way. Today, the American Catholic school system is the largest non-state school system in the world! Built and maintained from out of the wages of the poor, in 10,776 elementary schools, 2,432 secondary schools, and 282 colleges, it now enrolls 5,971,720 young Americans. From precarious beginnings it has successfully obtained for itself a prominent and significant place on the American scene.

The Catholic school system has not remained unchanged over the years. From the time of its founding following the Council of Baltimore and through the critical maturing years of the American Catholic community, the school system admirably performed the variety of tasks assigned to it, changing as the needs of the community changed. It served to protect the Faith: in its early years it served to preserve the traditional culture of various immigrant groups. As the Catholic community expressed its will to take on the coloration of the new land, it served to assist in the process; as the immigrant people sought social, economic, and political advance, it provided the schools and training needed.

Critics over the past few years have lamented the failure of Catholic education to produce great intellectuals. While it might be pointed out to these critics that it is rare for intellectuals to come out of a community whose attention is riveted on other goals, this would not be the total answer. Critics fail to take into cognizance the fact that the forming of intellectuals was not the task assigned to the Catholic schools by their constituency. The Catholic schools, up until the Second World War, basically were defensive institutions. In preserving the Faith, in giving new hope to a downtrodden people, in forming economically competent citizens, the schools served the needs of the people and of the nation. They formed responsible citizens for Church and State.

There can be no doubt that the Second World War marked a time of change for the Catholic community and thus for the schools serving that community. Nourished from infancy through adolescence within the protective walls of the Catholic school, the Catholic community now has reached its majority and has stepped forth to take up its rightful place within the nation. Recognizing this change in role, Catholic educators have undertaken the difficult and often painful process of reassessing, of re-evaluating, and of re-thinking needed for the making of changes in the established institutions. The Catholic schools are changing; indeed, they have changed. There is every reason to be confident that as they served well in the past, they will serve well the new, mature community. There is every reason to be confident that the future graduates will provide on every level the kind of leadership that Church and country have a right to expect of them in this very difficult age.

Before proceeding to any discussion of the major problems confronting Catholic education today, certain observations, drawn from history and philosophy, should be made. History establishes that there never has been *one American way* in education. The realization of the American dream was not brought about by the secular public school. The secular public school has newly come upon the scene. Educationally speaking, the American dream found its realization through diverse school systems—Protestant parochial, independent private, and Catholic parochial.

If one were to speak of the American way in education it should be to say that the American way is the way of pluralism. This pluralism may not have come about by considered decision, but providentially it has been the pattern. The pluralism is providential because in offering several different kinds of education it has preserved for Americans the basic principle of freedom of choice in the education of the young. It has preserved for Americans the concept arising from Western civilization that parents have a right in education, and that, indeed, the Church has a right in education.

If there is one thing in respect to education that all Americans should fear, it is a unitary school system dominated by the state. The idea of state domination over education proceeds from a philosophy of government and of life alien to American traditions and having serious implications for American institutions. While the right of non-state school systems to exist was vindicated by the Supreme Court in the Pierce decision, powerful forces remained active, seeking either a reversal of that decision in law or in practice. Thus, it is said by educators and by government officials that non-state schools exist by privilege and sufferance. It is said that the state possesses the sole right in education. Those who wish to preserve the American tradition and those who are concerned with the consequences of a unitary school system must be made aware that the struggle has not been ended.

It must be insisted that the plural school systems of the United States exist by right and that no one system, be it state or non-state, exists by a uniquely American right. It might well be that the resolution of this conflict with respect to education will become the most significant development in American culture in the second half of this century.

The right of non-state schools to exist and the right of parents freely to choose in education are being challenged not only upon the philosophical and political levels, but they are being challenged also upon the immediate and pragmatic levels. This challenge is one that primarily involves the Catholic school system. The reason for this primary involvement on the part of the Catholic school system is that it enrolls almost ninety percent of non-state school enrollment, and thus it stands as the chief preserver of traditional American pluralism in education.

There can be no doubt that at this moment the very existence of the Catholic school system as traditionally conceived is threatened. The words "traditionally conceived" are important. Catholic schools traditionally have been in a very true sense *public* schools. They have drawn their student bodies from the entire range of the social structure. They have not limited their enrollment economically by the imposition of high tuition rates or intellectually by the establishment of high standards for admission. However, in spite of the valiant efforts that brought about a growth in Catholic education of 117 percent from 1941 to 1960, each year sees the Catholic schools enrolling a decreasing percentage of the total Catholic school-age population. Every year, thousands upon thousands of young people are turned away from Catholic school classrooms, and others do not even apply because it is known that there is no room. With the demand exceeding the system's ability to meet it, inevitably criteria have been established for selection. Such criteria, to be found economically in the form of prohibitive tuition or intellectually in the form of admission standards, cannot but be seen as destroying the traditional *public* nature of Catholic education.

There can be no doubt that if a solution is not found, Catholic schools, in the years that lie ahead, will become not public schools for the many but private schools for the exclusive few. This would represent the end of any true freedom of choice in American education. It would, in fact, give to *one* school system a monopoly in education. It would make a mockery of the Supreme Court's dictum in the Pierce case that parents have a right to choose the kind of education they desire for their young. A right that is a naked right is not a right at all. It, indeed, would be cynical to say that Americans have a right to choose in education; however, they may exercise this choice only if they are wealthy or brilliant. With the survival of Catholic education in its traditional sense at stake, the stark and crucial issue confronting all Americans is the preservation of pluralism in education and thereby a freedom of choice in education.

It may be asked why Catholic education faces such a crisis today. What are the peculiar problems that have created the crisis? First of all, there is the problem mentioned earlier—the problem arising from the unprecedented demand for Catholic education. While state education has had its problems with the population explosion, it should be remembered that in the period during which Catholic education was growing 117 percent, state education was expanding by only 42 percent. The Catholic community of the United States has evidenced in an overwhelming manner its conviction that a religiously oriented education is of grave importance. The Catholic schools have grown because the Catholic people freely have chosen such schools—have chosen *this* kind of education for their children.

The second problem is one bound up with the problem of expansion—that is, teacher shortage. Prior to 1941, almost all of the teachers in Catholic schools were religious. These religious were paid little or nothing. Today, the dramatic expansion of Catholic education has exceeded the supply of religious and one out of every four teachers is a lay person, and it is estimated that within this decade it will be one to one. Catholic schools find it difficult to compete with state education in the matter of salaries for lay teachers and, therefore, find it difficult to obtain qualified teachers and, indeed, in many instances, to find any teachers whatsoever.

A third problem is that which arises from the expansion of knowledge. It was not too long ago that once a teacher had been trained, little was needed in the way of further education. Today, in almost every subject-matter field drastic revolutions have taken place. It has become necessary to re-train teachers and to establish extensive in-service programs. Furthermore, the explosion of knowledge has been accompanied by new and expensive equipment into the classrooms. With its constituency already under strain from the cost of maintaining two school systems, where is the Catholic school system to obtain money for the re-training of teachers, for the in-service programs, for the purchase of electronic equipment?

The fourth problem arises from the fact that standards are rising in education. It was not long ago that two years of college was deemed to be sufficient for a teacher. Today, a minimum of five years is being asked, with more being urged. Again, with the growing complexity of society, schools are being forced to assume a multitude of tasks formerly performed by other elements of society. As the schools assume such tasks, as rooms and personnel become essential, financing and staffing become of concern. Over the years, Catholic educators have been proud of the fact that Catholic schools have maintained standards equal to or superior to their state counterparts. Today, overwhelmed by the very massiveness of the problem created by a lack of adequate financing, Catholic educators are deeply concerned over the possibility of maintaining such standards.

It would be impossible to discuss adequately the problem of pluralism in education, or the problem confronting Catholic education in particular, without touching on the federal aid controversy. Various propagandists for special reasons have taken this controversy out of its proper context. In respect to the federal aid controversy there are certain misconceptions that have been accepted as being facts by all too many. First of all, there is the misconception that a consensus exists concerning the need for massive financial intervention by the federal government in education. There is no such consensus among authorities or laymen. There is no such consensus on the factual need or lack of need; there is no such consensus concerning the effects of federal intervention on the schools. Respecting the latter, there is a considerable body of opinion to the effect that the ills of American education could best be cured by a review of the purposes of that education. However this may be, the record does show that no consensus exists. Therefore, it is quite wrong to assert that any group in opposing federal aid is opposing the betterment of the public or opposing what the American people want.

The second misconception is to be found in the contention that the issue of aid to religious schools, and to Catholic schools in particular, has been the sole, or even the main, cause of recurring defeats of federal aid legislation. Fortunately or unfortunately, neither Catholics nor Catholic education has this kind of power in the Congress. As one looks through the press and the *Congressional Record* it becomes obvious that many factors are involved in the defeat of the legislation. There are several powerful lobbies that consistently oppose federal aid. The Civil Rights issue is always a major factor. Conservative Democrats and Republicans, with their fear of a central government, have played their part. The "all or nothing at all" attitude of the N.E.A. and its satellites have antagonized many. Above all, there is evidence of an apathy concerning the issue among the people. Certainly, if the people truly wanted federal aid, at some point in the sixty years in which it has been before the Congress it would have been passed.

A third misconception is that the Catholic hierarchy opposes federal aid and that the hierarchy is willing to injure public education in order to gain its own way. Actually, the Catholic hierarchy has no position on federal aid as such. Catholic bishops in speaking out have asserted that federal aid is a political and economic matter. However, as is their duty as leaders of their people, the bishops have expressed their conviction that if federal aid is enacted, justice would demand that it be given equally to all school children. There has not been, and there will not be, opposition to public education. There is the positive presentation for the rights and needs of children in the non-public schools.

A fourth misconception is one which was given credence by President Kennedy. Take President Kennedy's remark that aid to non-state schools definitely is unconstitutional. While no one knows what the Supreme Court would do if a case were brought before it, the most competent authorities on constitutional law have explicitly written to deny that aid to such schools would be unconstitutional. Reference need only be made to the writings of Professor Kauper of Michigan, Professor Sutherland of Harvard, Professor Katz of Wisconsin, and Professor Kurland of Chicago. The basic issue is not one of the Constitution but one of public policy.

With such misconceptions eliminated, conversations concerning aid to the non-state schools can be conducted on a level of reason and a level of civility. As Catholics see the matter, the basic issues are whether American pluralism in education will be preserved; whether freedom of choice in education will continue; whether American parents will have the right to choose the education of their young; whether any system not dominated by the state will be permitted in the United States.

It may be that the American people eventually will decide that they do not wish aid to go to the non-state schools. However, in making this decision the issues should be presented to them in a clear manner and should not be clouded by misconceptions. There is one argument often used against the offering of aid to the non-state schools. It is that if such aid were given, non-state schools would increase and there would be consequent weakening of public schools. It is somewhat paradoxical that, in the name of democracy, people should be afraid of democracy. It would seem that those who take this stand are afraid to permit the people to have a choice. They are afraid that if the people are free to choose they will choose in a manner contrary to the prevailing order. Undoubtedly, however, there are serious questions and serious problems in the issue. It is to be hoped that they will be discussed objectively and that a resolution of the entire issue will be brought about in a spirit of justice and charity. Certainly, the genius of our country is such that equity can be maintained and traditional American pluralism preserved. On a very pragmatic level, America should be reminded that it cannot afford to ignore the quality of education being given to over six million young citizens. Conviction of conscience and a desire for freedom of choice have led the parents to choose a religiously oriented education for their children. It would be a tragedy not only for the children, but for the nation, if economic forces should be used to compel that system to offer an inferior education in the secular fields.

Finally, it should be remembered that the Catholic

schools are American schools. They are dedicated to providing for the nation loyal, patriotic, and well-educated citizens. They attempt to give to their students the best of preparation in the secular fields of learning. In addition, they attempt to impart to these students a knowledge of the things of God and to develop in them a love of virtue. In an age confronted with a crisis of the spirit, that which is needed in America is a strengthening of religious education and not a weakening. Not only Catholics but the nation and, indeed, the world have a stake in the future of Catholic education in our country.

DEAN M. KELLEY

Protestants and Parochial Schools

In their attitudes toward parochial schools, as in most things, Protestants are diverse. Some operate their own parochial schools—Seventh Day Adventists, Missouri Synod Lutherans, Christian Reformed, and some Quakers and Episcopalians. Others object to any and all parochial schools, particularly those of the Roman Catholic Church, on grounds that they are "divisive," "undemocratic," and subversive of the public schools. Most Protestants, however, fall between these two extremes; they recognize the right of independent schools to exist (on their own resources), and consider them probably all right for those who want them.

But there is a remarkable degree of unanimity across all these shades of the Protestant spectrum in the feeling that parochial schools (including their own) should not be subsidized by tax funds. There is greater agreement on this issue among Protestants (sometimes for the wrong reasons) than on almost any other issue of public concern. One small but significant exception to this pattern is the Christian Reformed denomination—a conservative body of 250,000 members which operates several hundred Christian day schools. These schools, unlike most other parochial schools, are actually owned and managed by groups of parents, not by the church.

71

Some Protestants oppose tax aid to parochial schools from a deep but irrational hostility to the Roman Catholic Church, rooted in the bitter experiences of bygone centuries (for which Protestants bear a share of guilt as well), plus just enough contemporary conflict to keep anxieties alive. It is very difficult for these Protestants to weigh the parochial school issue objectively. But there are many other Protestants whose outlook is more rational and objective, though their opposition to tax aid is no less determined. This article is an attempt to interpret their viewpoint as the writer understands it.

Those who have visited Roman Catholic parochial schools have found in the best of them a warm and winning atmosphere of Christian nurture and a pervasive concern for the development of every pupil. In the less admirable schools there can be an authoritarian rigidity of discipline which fosters some very unlovely attitudes under the veneer of outward respect for the priests and sisters. Like public schools, they are a widely varied lot. But they represent a monumental accomplishment, and if they were forced to close, the nation would be poorer—not in the sense so often urged, that they save the public money, but that they add a significant dimension to American pluralism, and serve as an alternative and corrective to the sometimes overweening pretensions of some public schools and the sometimes underweening achievements of others. But they do these things only so long as they maintain their uniqueness and independence. When the independent schools cease to be independent and become increasingly indistinguishable from public schools, they lose much of their claim to respect and admiration.

The hard-pressed patrons of parochial schools may feel that respect and admiration will not pay the growing numbers of lay teachers nearly as well as money, and may be willing to trade some of the former for some of the latter. But they should realize that the character of their schools is involved in such a trade. A school that is supported in any significant degree by public funds is to that extent a public school, and becomes subject to certain conditions that sooner or later will minimize the distinctive religious character of that school and thereby its usefulness to parents and the church in fulfilling the purposes for which it ostensibly was founded. Such conditions would probably include the following:

1. If the whole community is contributing through taxes to the operation of a school, no segment of the community so contributing can be rightfully excluded from admittance to, *or employment in,* such schools, if academically qualified. (Non-Catholic teachers and pupils would certainly attenuate the effectiveness of Roman Catholic schools in teaching the faith to the children of the faithful.)

2. Sectarian religious rites and requirements should not be imposed on non-member pupils and teachers in such a quasi-public school. (This would include use of religious images in classrooms, etc.)

3. If the whole community is contributing through taxes to the operation of a school, the community so contributing is entitled to participate in determining the policy of that school through duly elected representatives. (This would mean the election of public members to a parochial school board in proportion to the amount of tax funds contributed to the total budget.)

These consequences might be fended off for a longer or shorter time, but they are implicit in the logic by which this country operates: "no taxation without representation," "public control of public funds," and so forth. Sooner or later the logic would show through, and it would be seen that a "private" school supported by public funds is a contradiction in terms. Many of us who respect and appreciate the contributions of independent schools to our common life together want them to be and remain truly independent.

The plea of financial crisis made on behalf of Roman Catholic parochial schools elicits some sympathy from Protestants, though they do not thereby feel obliged to agree to the particular measures of relief proposed or demanded by Cardinal Spellman or the Citizens for Educational Freedom. But the case for the economic difficulties of parochial schools has not been entirely convincing for several reasons.

Why is it that only the Roman Catholic schools are feeling the pinch and demanding tax assistance? The Missouri Synod Lutheran and the Seventh Day Adventist parochial schools have no teaching nuns to rely on and must pay salaries to lay teachers for all of their classrooms, yet they are not asking for direct aid for their schools—in fact, they have consistently opposed it. The Roman Catholic spokesmen for tax aid have not yet explained why this is so, and until they do, their case will remain unconvincing.

If a plea of financial hardship is to be convincing it must be much more adequately documented than it has been thus far. The Roman Catholic Church is reputed to be one of the most extensive landholders in the United States—certainly its assets are foremost among religious bodies today. For it to be pleading penury on behalf of its schools is incongruous, if not ludicrous. The exact financial condition of the Roman Catholic Church is one of the better-kept secrets of our time. But if it is to come into the legislative arena seeking relief, it will have to document its need more clearly.

This is particularly true in respect to contributions from the membership of the Roman Catholic Church. Students of stewardship estimate that the *average level of giving among the laity of the Roman Catholic Church is significantly lower than among the Protestant laity,* even allowing for the (diminishing) difference between the economic status of Protestants and Roman Catholics. It is hard for Protestants to see why they should pay taxes for the undergirding of Roman Catholic parochial schools when Roman Catholics are not exerting themselves to maintain their Church and its schools at the level which Protestants have achieved in supporting their churches (and schools, where these exist). If the Roman Catholic Church wants to make its plea of hardship convincing, it must show that its members are pulling their weight proportionately with others in the community in supporting what their consciences require, before demanding that the whole community pitch in and help them. This has not yet been shown, and the burden of proof rests upon those seeking change.

To be sure, the burden of so-called "double taxation" does fall heavily on some individuals who are payers of both property taxes for public schools and tuition for parochial schools, but this class is much smaller than is sometimes claimed, since many parochial school patrons are not property-owners and many send their children to parochial schools that do not charge tuition but finance the schools from general parish funds. Even in the case of those paying both tuition and public school taxes, the claim of "double taxation" is fallacious, since in the U.S. no church can "tax" its members. If Protestants and other non-Catholics were to be taxed by the legislature for the cost of aiding Roman Catholic parochial schools, in addition to the taxes they already pay for public schools, this would be a *genuine* case of double-taxation.

Some of the hostility of Protestants toward parochial schools can be attributed to an unconscious defensiveness against Roman Catholics, who seem to take religious education more seriously than most Protestants do, and who are attempting a much more ambitious, if not more effective, curriculum. Most Protestant churches give proportionately much less of their resources to Christian education of the young than does the Roman Catholic Church. They tend to give greater emphasis and support (proportionately) to foreign missions or other modes of evangelism. There has been agitation in some Episcopalian and Lutheran circles for systematic parochial school construction in every parish, but this has met with only mild response. The Christian Day School movement has its ardent advocates among members of the National Association of Evangelicals (a conservative group of Protestant denominations numbering around 2,000,000 members), and is gathering some strength from the alleged trend to "secularism" in public schools.

But in the largest Protestant denominations (Methodist —10,000,000, Southern Baptist—10,000,000, United Presbyterian—3,200,000, United Church of Christ—2,300,000) there is as yet little enthusiasm for parochial schools, and not much more for part-time weekday religious education plans such as released-time or shared-time. Despite the vehement urging of their educational specialists, Protestants today cannot work up much zeal for Sunday schools, let alone for church schools between Sundays.

This may be due in part to inertia or entropy, but I think it is also due to an unconscious suspicion on the part of many Protestants that classrooms do not accomplish a great deal for the faith as they conceive it. In the Methodist and Baptist traditions especially, there is less emphasis upon an intellectual deposit of faith to be transmitted to the young, and more upon an experiential encounter with the Holy Spirit through the charismatic preaching of the Word primarily to adults and older adolescents.

One might observe parenthetically at this point that there is some re-evaluating of parochial education on the part of Roman Catholics today. Some are asking whether operating a separate system of church schools of general education at all age-levels really accomplishes what they desire. To my knowledge no studies have demonstrated that parochial schools—Protestant or Roman Catholic— produce value-systems, behavioral patterns, personality structures, or even church loyalties in pupils consistently distinguishable from those produced in public schools. One interesting study at the University of Chicago suggested that traits of "religiosity" found in pupils at certain Protestant fundamentalist parochial schools were produced not by the schools but by attitudes and expectations acquired in church and home, and that these were *equally present in pupils from similar homes and churches who attended public schools!* Whatever the merits of these studies, the case has not yet been made empirically that parochial schools accomplish anything significant or distinctive in proportion to the cost of maintaining them.

I personally think that the "results" of parochial education probably become apparent at later ages than current studies have examined—perhaps in the twenties and thirties and beyond, after the young adult begins to "settle down" and raise his own family. Then attitudes and behavioral patterns implanted in the parochial school may reassert themselves, particularly in institutional loyalty to the church. This is a reflexive rather than a reflective kind of religious "result," but it may be considered worth the cost by some churches, if it is indeed produced by parochial education—which has not as yet been demonstrated.

Whether a church chooses to employ its resources primarily for parochial education or for foreign missions or for door-to-door visitation evangelism, *it is engaged in perpetuating, promulgating, propagating its faith.* For the state to subsidize one church's mode of discharging this duty but not another's would be discrimination indeed. If Roman Catholic parochial schools should receive tax aid, so should Methodist missions at home and abroad, and so should Baptist revivals.

But Protestants are not seeking "equal aid" for their endeavors. *They want no tax aid for any church, even their own.* This is a matter of principle for them, though they have not always lived up to it (and in some parts of the world have not yet discovered it). It is a matter of principle for reasons both of religious liberty and of church independence.

Religious Liberty. "To compel a man to furnish contributions of money for the propagation of opinions which he disbelieves and abhors is sinful and tyrannical. . . ." (Virgina Act for Establishing Religious Freedom). There are not many ways in our modern world that a man can give his support to what he believes in. Our money economy enables him to contribute voluntarily of his resources through gifts to his chosen faith. If he is deprived of this free choice and this free action by the taxing power of the state, he has been conscripted in the service of creeds he has not chosen. We have had abundant experience of this forced labor for religion through the ages, and it has not redounded to the health of the church or the credit of the state. It was to escape this kind of involuntary servitude to established churches that many of the colonists (and later immigrants) came to these shores. It would be tragic to institute today in this country the condition they sought to leave behind.

Independence of the Churches. In addition to the important dimension of religious liberty that would leave every man free to choose his religious faith and support it as he sees fit, Protestants demand for their churches, and covet for *all* churches and religious bodies, full independence to serve the Lord of the Church as He commands, and no other master. In most instances where the church has accepted tax support or other privileges, the state has usually and eventually gained dominance over it. As one Roman Catholic scholar put it, "The Prince's use of the Church as a tool of the State is the Renaissance Disease. It is an abomination wherever it occurs, and it is bound to happen wherever the Church depends upon the State for support." The struggle of centuries over lay investiture of church officials, the political exploitation of the Inquisition by Ferdinand and Isabella and their successors—these and a hundred other instances should remind us that the church has little to gain and much to lose by an alliance with the state. Its only hope of preserving its independence is to stay as free as possible of entanglements with the state.

All that has been expressed in this article is predicated upon an assumption which most Protestants make, and which many Roman Catholics might not be disposed to grant: that parochial schools are primarily and essentially *religious* institutions, organic to and inseparable from the church which operates them. Many Roman Catholics insist that parochial schools—at least insofar as they concern the public—are primarily and essentially *educational* institutions, and that their educational function can be viewed as distinct from their religious function. "This is an educational issue, not a religious issue," insisted one Roman Catholic leader, to which a Protestant spokesman responded, "For us, it is a religious issue, not an educational issue. And we have principles of conscience about it that we want to have respected in the same way that we try to respect the conscientious principles of others. We intend to stand by these principles, and you would not respect us if we didn't!"

The claim that there are some "secular subjects" taught in parochial schools that could be aided by tax funds without subsidizing the teaching of religion was the subject of recent research by George R. LaNoue ("Religious Schools and 'Secular' Subjects," *Harvard Educational Review,* Summer, 1962). Taking only the most obvious and accessible evidence—textbooks, and the most "secular" subjects, science, mathematics, and language—the researcher showed that religious symbols, practices, and doctrines were inextricably interwoven even in textbooks on these subjects, not only as illustrative material, but often in the central content of the subject matter and its interpretation. How much more religious material could be introduced, and how much more effectively, by the teacher, the symbolism of the classroom setting, and the whole atmosphere which a parochial school is designed to foster? This endeavor is indeed proper and commendable as an enterprise of a church and its adherents. It is only when the whole population, including those of other faiths and none, is asked— and not only asked, but required by law—to support this teaching that it becomes objectionable.

But, some Roman Catholic spokesmen claim, attendance at parochial schools fulfills the requirements of the compulsory education laws; therefore, parochial schools serve a public purpose in providing general education; they are entitled to reimbursement for this purpose, at least to the extent which represents the taxes of that segment of the public whose children attend parochial schools. Whatever else such schools may accomplish of value to the church is no business of the public.

As indicated above, Protestants and many others find themselves unable to disregard the religious content, purpose, and ownership of parochial schools, and the courts of this nation seem to be of a similar mind. Recently an Oregon law under which public school textbooks were provided to parochial schools was struck down when it was shown that the books were used for a religious purpose through teachers' guides prepared by church authorities (Dickman vs. School District, Oregon City).

A recent analysis of Supreme Court cases by George R. La Noue in "Public Funds for Public Schools?" concludes that the Supreme Court has permitted the pupils attending parochial schools to receive state benefits given to all children *only if*:

1. No religious organization or school acquired new property because of state action;

2. No religious use was made of whatever is provided by the state;

3. The state keeps complete control over the administration and distribution of state benefits.

If this analysis is correct, very little encouragement is given to the assertion that the public need concern itself solely with the secular educational function of parochial schools. The courts have scrutinized the religious element very closely. At most, the Supreme Court has permitted parochial pupils to receive bus transportation (Everson) and general textbooks (Cochran) used by public schools. In no case has it approved the giving of tax funds to churches to purchase their own books or buses, let alone to build classrooms or pay teachers! And this is consonant with the repugnance Protestants and many others would feel if tax funds were to be used to build up the real estate, prestige, and other assets of one church in preference to others, or even of all churches.

However, there are possibilities of compromise which many Protestants might find acceptable. A true compromise is one in which *both* sides make some concessions without sacrificing essential principles. Most of the proposals that have been made by Roman Catholic spokesmen for tax aid to parochial schools are not compromises but the beginning of establishment. Even if such aid were to go to *all* parochial schools, we would have fallen into the precise pattern that Patrick Henry and others proposed for Virginia in their "Bill for Establishing Teachers of the Christian Religion"—*multiple establishment*—but which was prevented by Madison and Jefferson.

One possible avenue of compromise which should be pursued is making tuition paid for parochial education deductible in computing federal income tax. This would put tuition in the same category as the contributions made to the church, which support parochial schools in some parishes that do not charge tuition. This proposal has already gained the approval of Lutheran bodies, and has been introduced in Congress by several legislators.

Another even more promising possibility for easing the financial burden of the patrons of parochial schools without violating the principles of other citizens is the "shared-time" plan. If it is asserted that there are some subjects taught in parochial schools that are essentially secular rather than religious in content (as has been asserted by several Roman Catholic clergymen and attorneys), then there seems to be little reason why these "secular" subjects could not be studied in public schools. The present obstacle is an all-or-nothing policy in public education under which parents must accept 100 percent of the public school curriculum or else none of it. Advocates of "shared-time" are urging that parents should be able to choose *part* of the public school offerings for their children, and part of the offerings of private or parochial schools to complete the credits necessary for graduation. They would continue to pay tuition for the latter, but would obtain the former free. If half the curriculum could be taken in public schools, parochial schools would be able to accommodate twice as many pupils as they now do with the same facilities and faculty, and parents would pay half of what they now pay in tuition.

Like any viable compromise, it offers advantages to *both* sides. Protestants would have the opportunity to offer certain courses in general education with a religious interpretation, such as history, social studies, art, music, or literature, without having to undertake the whole range of the curriculum. All children would mingle for a part of their educational careers in a common (public) school under instruction and control, which would mitigate the present sectarian segregation imputed to parochial schools. It would also give their parents a more direct concern in the betterment of public schools.

No national religious body has as yet given approval to the "shared-time" proposal, although the Division of Christian Education of the National Council of Churches has authorized its exploration. "Shared-time" systems are in operation in several cities, and will be watched carefully by all who are concerned to end the present impasse in education over the parochial school issue. If it is ended, it will be by some such solution, which respects the principles of all parties and offers advantages to each.

MILTON HIMMELFARB

Jewish Sentiment

Everyone knows that most Jews oppose federal aid to parochial schools. Institutional pronouncements do not always
mirror popular opinion, but in Church-State matters
among Jews they do. This is all the more striking because
the central Jewish tradition clearly favors religious education and practice for non-Jews, provided their religion is
not pagan. That tradition used to be as much a part of the
popular consciousness as of the elite's learning.

When I was a boy my mother told me a story about my
grandfather in the old country, which I later discovered
had been told about more illustrious figures and which
should be reckoned as belonging to the folklore and psychology of the Jews of Eastern Europe. The story is that he
once engaged a peasant coachman to drive him to another
town. In a few miles they passed a church, but the driver
did not cross himself. My grandfather waited a while and
then, on the pretext of having forgotten something, told
the driver to return home. When they got back my grandfather dismissed him and explained to my grandmother:
"A peasant who does not cross himself does not believe in
God. What is to prevent him from murdering me when
we are alone in the woods?" One of the few spokesmen for
federal aid in the Jewish community—though he is not
really of the community—Rabbi Schneersohn, the vene-

rated leader of the Habad (Lubavitch) school in Hasidism, has reasoned that since to will the end must be to will the means, Jews should therefore support federal aid.

Yet only in a part of the Orthodox section of the Jewish community does one find some support for federal aid; and even there, it is due to the needs of the Jewish day schools, which is what we call our counterpart of the parochial schools. If the Jewish community supported the day schools more adequately, as by subventions from its welfare funds, I suspect that the Jewish voices raised for federal aid would be even fewer than they are now.

All of which means that a newer tradition has largely replaced the older one. And in fact, in these questions the effective tradition of most Jews today, not only in the United States but also practically everywhere else in the Western world, is a strong, rather unified set of beliefs and attitudes that have grown out of the history of the Jews in the past two hundred years or so, since the Enlightenment and the beginnings of Jewish civic equality.

It should not have to be said that to Jews the adjective Christian does not mean or suggest what it does to Christians. In ordinary usage among Christians, it often means good, moral, admirable; sometimes it can even be a synonym of human. That is why the apocryphal chairman of the Brotherhood Week banquet could say, "Protestants, Catholics, Jews—we're all Christians together." (When the late Warren Austin represented the United States in the U.N., he once declared that Jews and Arabs ought to be able to settle their differences in a Christian spirit.) Jews, on the other hand—out of their European memories, to be sure, more than their American experience—can think of another anecdote. Soon after the end of World War I, it is said, an American Y.M.C.A. secretary attached to a relief mission in Hungary was introduced to the regent, Admiral

Horthy. Told that the initials stood for Young Men's Christian Association, Horthy shook hands and said, "Glad to meet a fellow anti-Semite." For many years *christlich* in European politics usually meant, among other things, anti-Semitic.

In the French Revolution, when the more modern-minded Jews responded eagerly to civic equality, on the whole the Church and churchmen were against it. In England it is only a little more than a hundred years ago that the first Jew was allowed to take his place in the House of Commons, against Anglican opposition. England must remain a Christian nation and state, the argument went, and therefore no Jew should be an M.P. Since Cromwell readmitted the Jews, England has been a far more tolerant and pleasant place for them than almost any other European country, and it has been happily free of the Continental strife between *laïques* and churchmen. Yet to this day English Jews are especially quick to see the point of the old joke that the Church of England is not the nation at prayer, as the Anglican theory has it, but the Tory party at prayer; and even now few of them can bring themselves to vote Tory.

Before Hitler the most disillusioning and frightening thing that happened to the Jews of the West—and to those Jews of backward countries like Russia who aspired to the status of their brothers in the West—was the Dreyfus case. It turned Theodor Herzl, who had once thought of leading a parade of Jews to the baptismal font, into the founder of Zionism. In France the mob and the Right bayed for blood, while Throne-and-Altar Catholicism denounced the Jews as gnawing worms and the Republic as a Judeo-Masonic conspiracy to subvert true religion and sound morality. The Dreyfus case accounts in part for the kind of separation between Church and State that was established in France when the anti-Dreyfusards were discredited, and it reinforced the attachment of Jews throughout the West to strict separation.

In the United States itself it was to protest a Catholic act of persecution in Italy that Jews created their first nationwide organization, just before the Civil War. In Bologna, a Jewish child called Edgar Mortara was baptized by a servant without the knowledge of his parents. When they dismissed her, she told the authorities what she had done and the papal police took the little boy away. It was a world-wide scandal, but the Church, including the American hierarchy, closed ranks. Nothing could persuade Pope Pius IX to return the boy to his parents. (He died, a priest, in 1940).

Not long ago the rabbi of my congregation asked me to tell an adult study group why I believed that Jews should modify their dominant opinion on Church-State matters, which I think is becoming a bit anachronistic. After I had spoken, a normally kind and friendly man rose to answer me, but he was so upset that he stopped after a few sentences and ran out of the room. (He later apologized.) He was born and educated in Czechoslovakia, and has never forgotten the taunts and occasional beatings he suffered on the days when the clergymen came to give religious instruction in school.

Any Jew with immigrant parents is likely to have heard of the fear, and sometimes danger, that their communities had to endure in Holy Week and especially on Easter, and there are many of my generation who remember the hazards of walking home from public school past the Polish or Irish parochial school. Today, even those Jews who know about recent trends in Catholic thought have probably had occasion to regret the lag between the new spirit on top and actual practice in the parish. A few months ago I overheard my daughter's friend tell her that the Jews killed Christ—that was what she had learned in released-time religious instruction—and I cannot suppose that I am an exception.

And of course most Jews, like most other non-Catholics, are unhappy with the Church's record on issues like divorce and birth control.

All this is to explain why Jews are not convinced that what the Church does and teaches is necessarily good and why they are not enthusiastic about proposals that public funds should be used to strengthen the parochial schools. Are they anti-Catholic? They are suspicious of the Church, but they are not against Catholics.

In 1928, when an anti-Catholic binge was America's answer to Al Smith's candidacy, Jews gave him a large majority of their votes. In 1960, probably a higher proportion of Jews than of Catholics voted for President Kennedy, and certainly a higher proportion of prosperous Jews than of prosperous Catholics. Later, in New York City the Catholic Wagner first got more Jewish votes than his Jewish opponent in the Democratic primary, Levitt, and then more than his Republican Jewish opponent, Lefkowitz.

In the 1920's, when the very life of the parochial-school system was at stake and Catholics were contesting the Oregon statute which made public education compulsory, the Jewish community sided with them. Louis Marshall submitted to the Supreme Court an *amicus curiae* brief challenging the constitutionality of the statute; and in those days the Jewish community was said to be under Marshall law.

Anti-Catholicism, in Peter Viereck's famous aphorism, is the anti-Semitism of the liberals. If that is so, then Jews are not anti-Catholic. An anti-Semite is not a man who is skeptical of Judaism or the synagogue; he is a man who hates Jews.

It is not only that most Jews are to some degree repelled by, or negative to, the Church and parochial schools. There are also attracted by, or positive to, the public schools. They think public schools are good and desirable in themselves.

On the whole, the history of the Jews in the United States is a success story, and they know it. Most are a generation or two removed from immigrant origins, and in that short time they have done fairly well, having become a predominantly middle-class community. Education is what helped to make this possible. Jews have been particularly grateful for free, universal education in the United States because where most of their parents or grandparents came from, the government tried to keep them out of whatever schools there were.

But the American public school did rather more for its Jewish students than help them to get ahead in the world. It also helped them to become part of America and of American culture, with unexpected speed and completeness. And for that the Jews are doubly grateful to the schools.

In the early years of this century Henry James saw the Lower East Side and worried about the national and cultural future of America. By a singularly apt irony of history, the grandchildren of the immigrants who worried him—graduates of the public schools—are today captains of the Henry James industry. Jewish professors are no new phenomenon in the Western world. There were many in the Kaiser's Germany and later in the Weimar Republic, but in both Germanies there were no Jewish professors of German history or literature. Those subjects were too close to the German essence to be entrusted to Jews, who were told to concentrate on mathematics or biology or art history. In the United States, Jews now teach English literature and American history at some of our greatest universities. The difference is appreciated even by the many Jews who, if you asked them to identify Henry James, would guess that he was Jesse's brother.

For Jews, America is the open and hospitable country that it is because the public school expresses its true spirit. They see the public school as simultaneously an instrument for individual progress and the symbol of a benign, inclusive national ideal. They take *e pluribus unum* seriously and they take pluralism seriously, and for them the public school is a kind of quintessential America which has succeeded remarkably well in reconciling the two.

Which is why Jews do not want anything to weaken public schools, in principle or practice. But they fear that is what federal aid to parochial education would do. They go farther. A chief reason why most Jewish welfare funds do not subsidize Jewish day schools is the common feeling that that would be a betrayal of the public schools.

Actually, it is on this point that the Jewish day-school movement differs most revealingly from the Catholic parochial school system. Everyone knows that the United States is where Catholic schools are for all Catholics rather than for an elite minority, and where half of the bold ambition to have every Catholic child in a Catholic school has already been achieved. That is an impressive ambition and an impressive achievement. It is quite otherwise with the Jewish day schools. They are rather new in having any statistical significance at all and they enroll fewer than ten percent of all Jewish children in school. What is more, the very advocates of the Jewish day schools do not dare, or do not even wish, to think that most Jewish students will attend them. The day schools are for a minority, a kind of saving remnant. Some of the warmest words I have ever heard for the public school, an institution and ideal, were spoken—sincerely, I am convinced—by an Orthodox rabbi who presides over one of the largest and best Jewish day schools in New York.

Many parents of day-school students express something akin to guilt over not sending their children to a public school, as well as explicit regret for the educational loss that their children incur by not being there. (So do many Jewish parents of children in non-sectarian private schools.) The guilt is because they fear they are helping to weaken the public schools. The regret is because in a public school their children would be learning, directly and by personal experience with children of various sorts and origins, what pluralism is and how to live in a pluralist America. Day-school educators answer that they are careful to teach understanding and respect for all religions, races, and nationalities. The educators do not question the principle, they merely do not like to think that they go against it.

There is an old Jewish story that I shall permit myself to tell. A rabbi, in his judicial capacity, heard a plaintiff and said that he was right. Then he heard the defendant and said that *he* was right. When the rabbi's wife protested to him that they could not both be right, he told her that she was right too.

I think that the parochial schoolers are right and that fairness, an ungrudging acceptance of Catholics as real equals in the American community, and the educational needs of the American people require public aid to parochial schools. I also think that the public schoolers are right and that the public schools have deserved well of the country, should be defended in their integrity and primacy, and might be threatened by measures that would make it easy, or almost painless, to expand the non-public sector.

The rabbi and his wife agreed that both sides could not be right. Must that be true also of the two sides in the dispute over federal aid, or can we help the parochial schools without hurting the public schools? For such a solution to be at all possible, as I hope it is, people will first have to give up self-righteousness and familiar and comforting watchwords.

I have not spoken here of constitutional arguments, though the friends and enemies of federal aid are fond of them. I know practically nothing about constitutional law, and I suspect that I am not alone in my ignorance. From what I have observed, even those who speak with knowledge are apt to be advocates rather than jurisconsults—that is, they advance legal arguments to defend ends and values which engage their loyalty on other than legal grounds. That is natural and honorable, but not persuasive. For myself, I assume that if we can arrive at a consensus on what is just and is good for the country and its people, it is likely to be constitutional.

MARTIN MAYER

Aid—With Strong Strings

The legal situation—so long as we stay with what is known to be enforceable law—is very simple. Except in the South, which maintains separate notions of justice and equality, every state in the union has a compulsory-attendance school law, with cut-off ages ranging from 14 to 18. (Even the Southern states had such laws prior to 1955, though none of them was of great antiquity; the earliest Southern universal education laws were a product of Reconstruction, and Mississippi did not get around to compulsory schooling until 1918.) Because the state requires children to go to school, and will put parents in jail for failure to send children to school, the state must make a determination as to what institutions qualify for the noble label "school." Municipal governments, too, under powers delegated to them by the states, can close schools, church-related or otherwise, for failure to maintain the minimum standards required by fire-prevention and health laws. Thus, every school must enjoy a degree of both state and municipal approval before it can operate.

This approval cannot unreasonably be denied: the Supreme Court in the Oregon case (1922) determined that a state cannot force all children to attend public schools. States do have, however, a wide latitude in the standards they may require private schools to meet before accepting attendance at such schools as compliance with the law. States can demand, though most of them don't, that all teachers be specially qualified, whether they work in public or private schools; or they can require, as California recently did, that all elementary schools, public or otherwise, teach a foreign language from grade four. Provided that the standards applied are not discriminatory against private institutions as such, states can make almost any rules they like governing the conduct of schools. This state power is inevitably inherent in *any* compulsory-attendance law.

At the same time, states subsidize all schools, except the occasional profit-making proprietary school. Ownership of real property, which is registered by the state and protected by the police, carries an obligation to pay taxes. Schools (and churches) are exempted from this obligation, on grounds of public policy. Others must therefore pay higher taxes, to make up for the revenue lost by the removal of school property from the tax rolls. The size of this subsidy, especially in big cities, is rarely realized. There are diocesan, Jesuit and independent schools in New York where the excused taxes add up to more than $100 per pupil per year; and in Boston, where the tax rates are monstrous, the figures are probably higher.

The federal government itself subsidizes private and church schools by allowing people who give them money to deduct the contribution from their taxable income. Tuition fees, however, are not deductible; and one New York independent school which tried to make a tuition increase more palatable by billing it as a "compulsory contribution" was rather firmly rebuked two or three years ago by the Internal Revenue Service.

In many states, goods and services—particularly textbooks, transportation and health services—are supplied from tax revenues to both public and private schools.

Sometimes, as in the various free-lunch programs, the costs of this state support are met by federal grants-in-aid. The theory here is somewhat different; the argument is that the assistance goes to the student, not to the school. As Glanville Williams once wrote about the doctrine that a doctor may legitimately give a terminal patient a fatal dose of morphine provided his intention is pain-killing rather than man-killing, this is the sort of thing that gives casuistry a bad name. Obviously, in a school supported primarily by fees from the parents, any grant to cover ancillary expenses releases money for the school itself. Such grants from state tax revenues, however, have been exposed to the litmus paper of the Constitution, and the Supreme Court has noted that it did not turn color. So states may or may not make such grants to private schools, depending on the legislative view of correct public policy.

At present, then, states control and subsidize private and church schools, to different degrees in different places. There are respectable arguments to be made for the proposition that government control and support of private schools has gone as far as public policy should carry it, that further control would endanger freedom or further subsidy would promote divisiveness, etc. In talking of federal aid at large, there is a case to be made against poking the camel's nose any further into the tent—we have had truly horrific experiences with the Smith-Hughes Act, which enabled a classically stupid but politically resourceful federal bureaucracy to prevent any improvement in vocational education. But there is no merit whatever to arguments which rest upon the assumption that state control and support of private schools, subsidized by federal grants, would introduce a new element into American polity. Both precedents and institutions already exist. The issue is whether or not extension of such institutions is sound public policy; and if we think it is, we should certainly proceed to extend them, allowing the justices of the Supreme Court, whom we pay for just such work, to decide whether the Constitution permits the policy.

Over the last quarter of a century, the American people have gigantically increased their financial support of education. In 1940, our total expenses on education ran about four percent of our national income; today, they run about six percent. Despite the series of quantum jumps in the number of children in school, we have in every year since the war increased (in constant dollars, allowing for inflation) the amount we spend *per pupil* in our schools. This remarkable accomplishment has been obscured by the persistence of the propaganda about "starving education," which was honest enough twenty years ago but has begun to acquire overtones of special interest. The desire to spend more money on education is now a matter of rational preference rather than demonstrable urgency; but the preference *is* rational. To function effectively, the next generation will need more and meatier education than today's American adults enjoyed or suffered through. And, generally speaking, more education costs more money.

A decline in the growth rate of the economy, however, has made it more painful to maintain the steep ascent of expenditure on education, and local tax rates, which create incentives for revenue sources to move to other localities, have been bumping the ceiling of the politically feasible. Meanwhile, increasing fluidity of motion from state to state has demonstrated, sometimes distressingly, the significance of a gap between annual expenditures of nearly $600 per pupil (in states like New York and Alaska) and expenditures of less than $300 per pupil (in states like Mississippi and South Carolina). At the same time, in education as in housing, local resources have been unable to

reverse or even arrest the catastrophic decline of our central cities; and a tentative movement toward curriculum
reform has shown that the ideational and technical difficulties of education are national in scope.

For one of these reasons or for all together, the majority
of Americans have come to support federal aid to education—sample surveys consistently draw Yes answers from
three-fifths or three-quarters of those who have an opinion.
Their desire, presumably, is to see our schools operating
at a higher average level of competence and efficiency.
Having looked fairly hard at American education for more
than five years, I am a little dubious about the degree to
which this purpose can be achieved merely by pumping
money into the existing bureaucracy.

Francis Keppel, our new Commissioner of Education,
also seems to doubt the value of buckshot federal aid; the
bill he proposed to the current Congress, which is still
pending, directs the silver bullets at specific targets (curriculum reform movements, special teacher training,
higher salaries for career teachers, experiments in the
slums). Keppel has had the courage to admit that federal
aid must imply a degree of federal control—the hand that
pays the piper rules the world. Under the new bill, however,
this control is to be exercised only through the states,
which are to prepare their own proposals for the use of the
money and then see to it that expenditures on the local
level match the purposes of the grant.

Now, as a matter of sheer formal structure, money allo-
cated to the states for specific purposes can be spent in
private schools as easily as in public schools. Indeed, one
of the titles in the pending bill—to encourage the development of new materials and methods of instruction in academic subjects, and to train teachers to handle the new
courses—would open the federal purse to private and

church schools. The rest of the titles, as they affect education below the college level, are restricted to benefit public
schools alone.

I have supported this bill as it stands, and I am among
those who believe that the Catholic hierarchy's public
opposition to it—particularly in the case of Cardinal Spellman—reflects a political objection to federal aid in any
form more than a special objection to the exclusion of
the church-related schools. I would happily join the
N.C.W.C., however, if it would support amendments
which made federal money available to private and church
schools under all the titles of this or any succeeding act—
*provided that this money would be spent only under tight
state control.*

Practical reasons of efficacy rather than theoretical reasons
of fairness underlie this position. Many parents, particularly
Catholic parents, wish their children to be educated in
a religiously-controlled environment, and the decision
in the Oregon case assures their right to fulfill their
wish. *Pace* Conant and P.O.A.U., then, some millions of
American children will receive their education in church-
related schools. If there is a national interest in improving
educational standards, it extends to the education of these
children, too. The logic of the compulsory-attendance laws
argues that we must demand from church-related schools
whatever improvements in quality we are able to achieve
in the public schools.

By and large, though our evidence will continue to be
scanty until Father Hesburgh and Dr. Shuster publish
their report, the Catholic schools seem to be a depressed
area in American education. By whatever objective meas-
urements we can make, they rank well below the public
schools of their areas. Less money is spent per pupil, class
sizes are substantially larger, there are fewer teachers per

thousand pupils, and the teachers themselves are typically less well prepared (which is saying a good deal). As Monsignor Ellis, Father Weigel and Professor O'Dea have pointed out, the Catholic community has not been contributing to the intellectual leadership of the country in anything like the quantities its numbers would lead us to expect—and while this deficiency doubtless has complex roots, it must bear some relation to the simple quality of the Catholic schools.

There are far too many places where Catholic education is in fact "parochial"—where the schools are controlled by parish priests who may have neither competence nor interest in education other than the Sunday-school variety. Though there are good diocesan school systems, and excellent parochial schools, the average level seems considerably lower than it should be. In my rather limited observation, the level of Catholic education seems lower than the level of public education, allowing for all the bumps up and down from average in both categories.

In this situation, control by competent authority over the expenditure of tax moneys is absolutely essential. Many of the strains on Catholic education are the result of helter-skelter expansion since the war. Any legislation that simply donated funds to church-related schools might promote further random expansion. If I am right in believing that Catholic schools are on balance inferior, public policy certainly should not promote their expanison. *If public money is to be made available for church-related schools, it must be spent to improve the education of the existing pupil population, not to increase the numbers of children in such schools.*

It seems to me, then, that what the Church should request is money to reduce class size, to hire additional teachers, to improve facilities, to introduce the new materials and methods now being developed under grant from the foundations and from federal bodies like the Office of Education and the National Science Foundation. To qualify for public support, the Church should declare that in whatever units are accepted as appropriate—state, city or diocesan—if will not seek to increase the number of pupils in its schools until these schools have become by some objective criteria (average class size, for example, or pupil-teacher ratio) at least the equal of the neighboring public schools. Existing mechanisms of state control and amended mechanisms of state support could then be employed to channel tax revenues into private schools for the national good.

If the Catholic bishops will make such a request to the Congress, there are, I think, many non-Catholics like myself who will fight beside them. There might even be enough of us to amend the Constitution, if the Supreme Court says that such an amendment is required. Historically, once we as Americans have decided what we ought to do, the genius of our political system has permitted us to do it. The real question here is not the arid business of law and political principle, but the moist, warm, human stuff of the nation's children; what we should be debating is the possible benefit to them, not the possible comfort to some secular or clerical bureaucracy.

JOHN G. DEEDY, JR.

The Shared-Time Experiment

In twenty-six or more communities across the nation, communities as distant and disparate as Bangor, Maine, De Witt, Iowa, and Salem, Oregon, several hundred parochial school students are engaged in one of the most interesting experiments in American educational history. It is an experiment which could measurably ease the private and parochial schools' crisis of facilities, funds and teachers. But at the same time this experiment could create enormous problems for the public school; and, if it develops to the fullness of possibilities, it could set American education—private, parochial and public—on a totally different course, almost overnight, from that which has evolved over a century and a half. For good reasons is the experiment being watched with feelings which range the emotions. Some people are optimistic, hopeful, even prayerful; some are cynical, dubious, apprehensive, antagonistic.

The experiment, of course, is shared-time education, a program whereby the private or parochial school pupil on the junior high or high school level receives a portion of his education at his private or parochial school and a portion at the public school of his residency district. Because ninety percent of the enrollment in non-public elementary and secondary schools in the United States is in Catholic schools, the shared-time discussion in its present context

103

fixes upon Catholic and public school authorities. Whether the fact is welcome or not, this gives the discussion a religious focus which is almost exclusively Catholic and which, by the same token, may be a distortion so far as the future is concerned. For not only is shared-time more Protestant than Catholic in its inspiration, it also holds a potential for any number of groups or movements besides the strictly religious, Catholic or otherwise.

Shared-time is not a new concept. A 1963 study prepared by the legislative reference service of the Library of Congress states that limited shared-time programs have been in operation for forty years or more; actually the City of Pittsburgh has known a shared-time course in practical arts since 1913. The idea is even older. The shared-time notion, though not specifically titled such, is discernible, for instance, in the arguments of some of those opposed to the establishment of an independent Catholic school system in nineteenth-century America. But it is only in very recent years that the program has moved beyond the theoretical or modified stages and into the realm of pure shared-time, where the school hours of the student are divided (or shared) in time proportion and subject importance between the parochial and public schools of the student's enrollment.

As might be expected, most, if not all, of the schools participating in shared-time are Catholic. Yet, surprisingly enough, the shared-time experiment is precisely where it is because of a series of recent Protestant initiatives. Perhaps the first of these was the publication in 1956 of Erwin L. Shaver's much discussed book *The Weekday School Church* (Boston, The Pilgrim Press, 1956), in which were outlined the advantages of "the growing practice in many communities throughout America of having children, whose primary enrollment is in a parochial school, take some of their courses in the public school." Another initiative would certainly be the writings and lectures of Dr. Harry L. Stearns, superintendent of schools in Englewood, New Jersey, and a member of the Board of Christian Education of the United Presbyterian Church, U.S.A.; it was he who coined the phrase "shared-time" and who inaugurated the private meetings among churchmen and educators that have strongly influenced shared-time trends since 1960.

These meetings, incidentally, turned up three schools of thought on shared-time education. One school (Protestant and Catholic) saw shared-time increasing the religious literacy of America's children; a second (Jewish and Protestant) took a sociological view and envisioned shared-time as a bridge over divisiveness; a third (Protestant, Catholic and Jewish) approached shared-time as the answer to the federal aid to education impasse. Whatever the logic, balance, legitimacy or validity of the individual schools, it was the Catholics who put shared-time to the test, thus moving discussion from the conference rooms and the journals of opinion into the arena of actuality.

In Monroeville, Pennsylvania, outside Pittsburgh, some thirty-six students from three Catholic high schools were soon spending half their school day at Forbes Trail Area Technical School for courses such as marketing, chemistry, computer training and maintenance, engineering and automotive technology, and half their day at their Catholic school studying Christian Doctrine, social sciences, English, mathematics and languages. In suburban Detroit, two-hundred seventh and eighth grade pupils of a parish school moved to Cherry Hill Junior-Senior High School for mathematics, science, physical education, home economics and shop training. In Bay City, Michigan, thirty-eight students from St. Joseph High School began to pursue trigonometry, drafting, vocational education, Spanish and homemaking at one of that city's public high schools, and twenty-five students from St. Mary's High took mechanical drawing, shop and homemaking at a second public school. The pattern repeated itself in several other localities, including St. Paul, Saginaw, Toledo, Hartford, Philadelphia, Springfield, Missouri, and Flint, Michigan. Exactly how many cities are involved in shared-time education is not known. The Education Department of the National Catholic Welfare Conference in Washington, D. C., is keeping a file on such programs, but it only knows those which have come to its attention through newspaper clippings. That office's count of shared-time cities stands at twenty-six, most of them with post-1961 arrangements.*

The astonishing aspect about the shared-time arrangements to date is the degree of their administrative success. Of course the programs are limited and of course there have been problems. In Philadelphia, for instance, there is a question over transportation of students, but at the other end of Pennsylvania, Braddock-area students are picked up at the public school nearest their parochial school, driven several miles to a public school in Monroeville, and then transported back to the public school point of origin. All things considered, shared-time has worked well and the dire predictions of the pessimists have not materialized. Public and parochial school administrators have demonstrated that cooperation is possible; schedules have been

* Maurice J. Thomas, professor of education and chairman of the program in educational administration at the University of Pittsburgh, declared at the February, 1964, conference of the American Association of School Administrators in Atlantic City that some one hundred and fifty communities are experimenting with shared-time and that the number increases each year. He said that Michigan, Ohio and Pennsylvania have the most shared-time experiments.

harmonized; students have adjusted to differing systems and codes; resentment has been minimal; constitutional challenge is still absent.

Yet as problems and worries have vanished one by one, a larger and infinitely more urgent question has cropped up. This question is not whether shared-time will stand the inevitable test of constitutionality. (C. Stanley Lowell declared in a telephone conversation recently that legal probes from P.O.A.U. are quite possible.) Nor is the question whether shared-time will eliminate aid-to-education conflicts or contribute to the democratization of society; or whether shared-time will promote the religious literacy of a substantially larger portion of the population; or whether shared-time will guarantee the survival or increase the potential of private and parochial schools. *The big question is what shared-time might do to the public school system.* Will the public school be able to cope with the challenge of a broad or total shared-time educational system without its character and its program being warped and its service to the general citizenry being diminished by the necessity of meeting the demands of the group? Will the pubic school, so distinguished a part of the American past and so invaluable to the nation's future, be fragmented by shared-time so that its effectiveness will be reduced and its potential diminished?

These are the overriding considerations, but they seem not yet to have been sufficiently taken into consideration. There are great emphases on the advantages of shared-time and these advantages are real and much to be desired. (They are also well-known, especially to readers of the Catholic press, so anxious to solve the parochial school's problems that it has a tendency to view all possible avenues of relief through the rosiest of glasses.) But there is a dearth of discussion about the harmful effects shared-time could have on the public school; these are menacing and could prove disastrous.

The fragmentation of public schools by shared-time has disturbed a few parties. The *Christian Century*, distinguished Protestant-oriented weekly, and the Commission on Law and Social Action of the American Jewish Congress, through its director, Leo Pfeffer, both have taken positions against shared-time on grounds of fragmentation. "The divorcing of history, the humanities, the arts and social studies—which the church schools would certainly want to preempt for their students—from the sciences, mathematics, athletics and manual training would create an intolerable dichotomy for both religious and secular educations," the *Christian Century* commented March 14, 1962. And Mr. Pfeffer wrote in the June 1, 1962, *CLSA Reports*: "We might end up in many communities with a situation where all the important subjects needed for human relations are taught in a multiplicity of separate religious schools and the public school used as a common manual training institution, physical science laboratory or gigantic gymnasium."

Mr. Pfeffer (an early advocate, by the way, of shared-time) advances nine reasons, some of questionable validity, for his new opposition to the program. But it is in the point cited here that he comes closest to the great cause for concern. The public school is a proud, honorable and vital institution; it is also a sensitive institution and would be vulnerable to a shared-time program which saw non-public half-schools (which shared-time invites) indiscriminately multiplied and students from these schools moved recklessly into the public school for courses which the non-public school found of prohibitive expense or neutral importance to bother with itself. Such an eventuality could speedily reduce the public school to little more than a scientific, dietary, athletic and recreational center.

Shared-time education is healthy and desirable, *but only within a framework which protects the public school's dignity and its quality.*

I am not suggesting that parochial school authorities are so callous or so contemptuous of the public school's place and tradition that they would wish to see the public school reduced to the status, as it were, of a service station. But this could be the public school's fate through a general and thoughtless shared-time program. Should this happen, the guilty parties, curiously enough, might not necessarily be the authorities of church-related schools. They could be unionists or political actionists or almost anyone else. For, remember, if it is constitutional for church-related schools to establish shared-time education programs, why not also union groups, political parties, or movements of sundry sorts? Even the John Birch Society could conceivably found its own school system, one in which students took their social, economic, political and history studies in the John Birch school and hopped over to the public school for neutral subjects. The thought seems preposterous, but the possibility is there so long as public school doors are open on a shared-time basis to students from church-related or any other type school.

Apropos fragmentation, it should be kept in mind that this is a two-edged sword, and that it is not just the public school, but the private and parochial schools too which could be decimated. The Catholic school system has been built up by fantastic effort and sacrifice. Right now it is going through a teacher and financial crisis. Shared-time not only dangles a lure to the overcoming of this crisis; it also baits the hope of doubling the number of pupils the schools now handle. But the cautious give pause—and not only because shared-time seems too perfect an alchemy.

The cautious urge pause: a) because it seems unlikely that the public is disposed to an educational arrangement which could radically change traditional public educational processes; and b) because there always lingers the possibility that the courts will rule against shared-time. There is presently no decision of the Supreme Court which is directly germane to shared-time, and none looms in the immediate future. In fact, the climate of law and of opinion at the moment seems favorable to shared-time. But who can predict a generation from now or two generations? If, in the meantime, the private and parochial schools have committed themselves totally or substantially to shared-time, and if the decision went against these schools, they could find themselves handicapped to the point of extinction. For by then they might be mere half-schools or maybe even catechetical centers, and it might be too late in the day to begin all over again.

We are not arguing in all of this that shared-time has no place in the American scheme of education; we are saying only that shared-time needs a perspective. Right now the experiment wanders in a forest of unanswered questions. How much shared-time do church-related groups, Protestant, Catholic and Jewish, expect? Are all public school subjects potential shared-time courses? Will the public authority allow shared-time arrangements to extend beyond religious groups? To what extent can the public school accommodate itself to shared-time without becoming a distortion? And what is the mind of the public, to whom the public schools belong? Answers to these questions seem essential, immediately so, if shared-time is not to grow, in topsy-turvy fashion, and then some day come crashing down on everyone concerned.

The answers can be had only after major influential

educational bodies—the National Education Association, the N.C.W.C. Education Department, the National Catholic Educational Association, the American Association of School Administrators and others—make known their minds on shared-time. Until now these associations have had no official stand on shared-time, and though this reserve may once have been prudent and necessary, if only to witness the preliminary testing of shared-time, the silence now becomes disconcerting.

PHILIP SCHARPER

Catholics and Public Schools

In 1848 waves of Nativists swept through Philadelphia, leaving in their wake churches burned and convents pillaged or destroyed. The occasion of this crusade was the objection publicly voiced by Bishop Kenrick that the Protestant climate of the public schools constituted a threat to the faith of Catholic students within them.

In 1955 the American hierarchy in its annual statement observed: "The rise and vigorous expansion of the American educational system is cited, correctly, as one of the major achievements of Western civilization. . . . It would be blind prejudice which would refuse to acknowledge, in this connection, the tremendous accomplishment of the public educational agencies."

In 1963 several major Catholic archdioceses announced a moratorium on further elementary school construction, and in its issue of September 15, *America* published a debate between two priest-educators on whether or not the American Catholic college is obsolescent.

These dates and facts are neat historical bench marks for the relation of Catholics in America to American public education. Confronted with the fact that the Protestant was the operative ethos in the public schools, the largely immigrant Church shaped its protest not only by establishing its own sectarian schools, but also by pushing its cause through the courts on grounds not too dissimilar from those of the professed atheists, Mrs. McCollum and Mrs. Madelyn Murray, a century later. By that later date, Catholics had been woven into the American fabric, and even though they could themselves provide a Catholic post-diaper to post-doctorate education, they could also share the general American feeling that public education in the United States represented a monumental achievement. By 1963, indeed, more and more Catholics were asking if public education were not generally so superior in funds and faculty that American Catholicism might well consider the wisdom of 1) diverting its own educational expenditures of personnel and money into other channels, and 2) letting public education prevail. Opposition, acceptance, assimilation: these form the triad of Catholic attitudes to public education, and account for an increasingly discernible division among American Catholics.

Many today assume that an attitude of active Catholic opposition to the public school is as anachronistic in fact as it is in theory, since the image of the public school as a Protestant institution no longer corresponds to reality. But many Catholics today fear the religious neutrality of the public education as much as their forbears feared its Protestantism; these Catholics deem public schools godless, just as thousands of Protestants continue to view the public school as "essentially compatible with Protestant theology."

The grounds for such continuing Catholic opposition are readily understood. Historically, Catholics felt both culturally and religiously alien to the public school, and hence did not participate in its life. Further, the Catholic school system was looked upon, from within and without, as a rival educational venture, and rivalry is but rarely the matrix of cordiality and cooperation. Even today a Catholic running for office on a school board may often be looked upon as a possible saboteur (or traitor) even though he is an American citizen and a local taxpayer as well as Roman Catholic.

Statistics, as well as history, provide a ground for still-active Catholic resentment or even active opposition to public education. Quite apart from its religious character, as a private school system Catholic education in the United States is a massive fact. Not only do Catholic schools exist in every state of the union, but in half of the states these schools educate more than ten percent of the state's students, and in ten states Catholic schools account for the education of twenty to twenty-five percent of total state enrollments.

Given the fact that such a heavy share of the nation's total elementary and secondary education is carried on by Catholic educators and parents without tax support, it is not surprising if occasionally tempers grow thin or patience snaps when the question of public funds for parochial schools is treated by some non-Catholics as though the sectarian education involved were that being offered to several hundred students by a splinter sect of the Mennonites. Further, the very effort to keep the massive Catholic educational effort moving so drains the time, energies and money of the Catholics involved—bishops, priests, sisters and laymen—that even where vestigial resentment of tax-supported schools has not been given new life by the federal-aid debate, Catholics are often too involved with their own problems to take an active interest in public education, either in their own communities or in the nation.

Given the fact of these pockets of Catholic resentment toward public education as a rival enterprise and of general Catholic indifference to public schools as a consequence of preoccupation with their own, it would seem to follow that these attitudes would result in a deliberate effort to weaken public education wherever Catholics were numerous enough to be the pivotal bloc affecting school bond issues or education budgets for the public system. Such a charge is easier to make than to substantiate, although the charge seems made often enough.

What few studies have been made suggest that the existence of a parochial system in no way affects the politics of financing public schools at the local and state levels. At a seminar sponsored in the Spring of 1963 by Syracuse University, Professor Miner of Syracuse described his statistical study of 1,100 school districts; his investigation revealed that communities spend just as much per public school child regardless of whether or not the Catholics in the community are also supporting large numbers of Catholic schools. At the same seminar, Dean Stephen Bailey of Syracuse's Graduate School of Citizenship and Public Affairs pointed out that in eight northeastern states parochial schools did not have an adverse effect on state aid to education—although, be it noted, in five of these states more than twenty percent of the state's students are enrolled in Catholic schools. Where public funds are inadequate to the needs of public education (and where are they not?) public apathy in general, and not Catholic opposition in particular, must bear the blame.

Far more significant than present opposition is the growing Catholic acceptance of the public school. "[It] is a respected and necessary national institution," begins a recent "white paper" on the Catholic Church and the public school prepared by a committee of Catholic diocesan school superintendents. The paper then continues: "If the reminder is needed for the few—the public school is here to stay. The choices then are simple. . . . The alternatives are either to support and strengthen a form of public education which, of necessity, will take place within a less than

perfect atmosphere, or to continue to promote by our indifference the purely secular school which we can then
continue to condemn for its godlessness."

The entire document is interesting for at least two reasons: it represents the most thoughtful "official" statement
to date of Catholic acceptance of public education, and it
bases that acceptance on the grounds of both pragmatism
("for this generation at least the goal of having the great
majority of Catholic children in Catholic schools is un-
attainable") and principle ("Catholic citizens have as grave
an obligation toward the common welfare as has anyone
else, and the concept of the common welfare today includes publicly supported education").

Regarding the pragmatic grounds, one can but suspect
the committee of a rush of optimism to its temples—un-
characteristic indeed of diocesan superintendents. The
goal of "every Catholic child in a Catholic school" was
unrealistic when uttered by the Third Plenary Council of
Baltimore in 1884—and it will be less, not more, realistic in
1984. To cite but one case (admittedly an extreme, but
not unique one), a current projection places the Catholic
population of Chicago at 3.3 million by 1985 in contrast to
its 2.2 million in 1960. Educationally, the projection fore-
sees from 1960 to 1985 an increase of seventy-eight percent
in the number of children requiring some form of Catholic
education. This increase would suggest that one hundred
new high schools must be built by 1985 if the Archdiocese
of Chicago is to educate the same proportion of the high
school age population as it did in 1960.

In the national scale, the projections are not better calculated to comfort the shades of the Council Fathers of
1884 than is the Chicago projection. By 1985 approxi-
mately seventy-five percent of the Catholics in the 18-24
age bracket may be in non-Catholic colleges and univer-

sities, while at least one projection suggests that eighty to ninety percent of high-school-age Catholics will not be in Catholic schools. American Catholics, then, are coming to accept public education for the same reasons which ultimately forced Margaret Fuller to accept the universe.

Granted the fact of acceptance, however, one must question what level and mood of acceptance there will be. Recurring to the superintendents' statement of principle (" . . . the concept of the common welfare today includes publicly supported education") one can but applaud its appositeness yet worry about its effective application by a large segment of the American Catholic community.

Consider but two areas of strategic importance where Catholic collaboration is needed and might even prove decisive: the present financial needs of public education, and the religious illiteracy which is too often the by-product of the tax-supported school.

The first area, the poverty of the schools within an allegedly affluent society, needs little documentation. New York City, with more public school pupils than Baltimore has people, holds four or five daily shifts in some of its high schools. One Maryland county was forced to hire eighty inexperienced teachers when its school budget was cut by $500,000. In both urban and rural slums, schools have had to cut out "frills"—such as languages (including Latin)—or to have class ratios of eighty pupils or more per teacher. Education under these conditions, it has been observed, does little more than keep children out of the rain—and in the decaying schools of some large cities it fails to do even that.

Ironies abound in a situation such as this. While there is a palpable classroom shortage throughout the nation, public officials, labor leaders, economists and educators are joined in a national campaign to stem the tide of "dropouts" and even return the strayed to the fold—if one can be found. In Washington, D.C., in the summer of 1963, hard-working school personnel and volunteers persuaded 800 dropouts to return to school. But Congress, over that same summer, had failed to consider an urgent request for additional funds to hire 344 new teachers. How can the dropout—actual or potential—be expected to take education seriously when so many of his elders do not?

The nation's educational slums are spreading through neglect, and the neglect is caused in great part because too many citizens fear the costs necessary, not for educational excellence, but for adequacy. The nation pays a heavier but hidden bill, of course, for educational neglect: in rejection for military service, in low earning capacity, in chronic unemployment of the unemployable, an appalling outlay for relief, and the economic burden of crime and delinquency.

"Withered be the hand raised against the public school," once exclaimed the late, great Archbishop Ireland of St. Paul. But few now would raise their hand against the public school. The present threat is that too many will keep their hands in their pockets, knuckles white against the money clip.

These previous paragraphs have been a long, but I trust not pointless preamble to what I would regard as a badly needed contribution which American Catholics might reasonably make to help solve the financial crisis of public education. This crisis, in all probability, cannot be solved without federal funds being generously provided for public education. The federal government presently receives more than two-thirds of all tax revenues, but pays only 3.6 percent of the nation's school bill, whereas the local communities pay 39.4 percent. On the local level, it is becoming clear that real estate taxes can no longer support the schools even in the manner to which they have become accustomed, let alone build, equip and staff the public schools to meet the quantitative and qualitative demands of the next decade.

Yet the provision of federal funds for public elementary and secondary education has been stalled by a coalition of factors, principally a conservative opposition to any federal assistance to education, the opposition of some Negro groups to federal aid to segregated schools, and Catholic opposition to federal aid unless parochial schools are included.

If, to quote again the Diocesan Superintendents' statement, "Catholic citizens have as grave an obligation toward the common welfare as has anyone else, and the concept of the common welfare today includes publicly supported education," it is hard to see why the moral support of American Catholicism should not be thrown behind, rather than against, the provision of federal funds for public education, without present consideration of whether or not parochial schools were to be included in such aid. The same line of reasoning, be it noted, would suggest that the high demands of the common welfare might prompt Negro groups to drop their opposition, and fight their cause for integrated schools on other, clearer ground.

The exact mode in which this Catholic support should be voiced is less important than that it be voiced—above a whisper or a grudging statement. Obviously, a ringing declaration by the American hierarchy, or by significant groups of bishops, would proclaim that Catholics are, in the *agora* as in the academy, philosophers of the common good. But such highly official action is not necessary, effective though it would be. Catholic groups of every purpose —fraternal, charitable, spiritual—on every level from the national to the parochial, might well analyze the question of federal aid in terms other than what are usually thought "Catholic interests." Even if loftier motives were not to prevail, the sober calculation of the number of Catholic children in public schools in the present and future would bring the realization that, in this instance, Catholic interests are largely coincident with those of public education.

It need scarcely be pointed out that Catholic support of federal aid to education does not weaken the wide-spread Catholic view (which I share) that religiously oriented schools are also entitled to such aid. Indeed, both points of view rest on the same premise: that the proper education of its citizens is a primary concern of democratic government, and hence education has a right to governmental support when the sponsoring agency—state, municipality or religious group—cannot completely pay for that level of education which is in the best interests of the government itself.

In the clamorous crises which have beset America—wars, the upward struggle of labor, the current civil rights revolution—Catholics have made notable contributions. The financial crisis of the public schools is a quiet one; large sectors of the populace are numb or apathetic. "Nobody ever died of a split infinitive," remarked U.S. Commissioner of Education Francis Keppel when asked why it is so hard to arouse the public to the needs of its schools. American Catholicism could render a great national service if its voice were raised, above the complacent chatter, in strong support, moral and financial, of the American public school.

Obviously, the public schools are faced with other problems for which money cannot provide the solution. Paramount among these is the question which has flared into prominence as a result of the Supreme Court's decisions on prayer and Bible readings in the schools: is the public school now powerless to teach "moral and spiritual values" in the context of the Judaeo-Christian tradition? Will the public schools become, of necessity, secular institutions?

Judging from the quoted comments of Catholic officials and Catholic editorials on these Court decisions, one would have to conclude that many, perhaps most, American Catholics probably think that an irreversible trend has set in, and that, as a consequence, public education is becoming totally secularized. (Many non-Catholics share this view, of course, but are not the immediate concern of this article.)

To attach such value to largely symbolic acts as recitation of the Lord's Prayer (or the Regents') and a Bible reading without commentary is, perhaps, to concentrate on the first five minutes of the school day and to overlook what can be done with the rest of it. Prayer, as such, did not and could not come under the Supreme Court's collective gaze, but, to my knowledge, little attention was paid to that fact by those who felt, with the New York *Daily News,* that God was "booted out of the classroom when recited prayers and Bible reading went the way of Webster's Blue-Backed Speller."

Could not a diocese, or a C.C.D. unit, or a parish, or a Holy Name Society print and distribute to its Catholic students in public schools book marks for private use, containing appropriate prayers and ejaculations, or even a set of cards keyed to each of the major subjects studied? Such a simple device might even encourage *prayerfulness,* which the common recitation of the Lord's Prayer seemed scarcely calculated to bring about. In areas where the ecumenical climate was clear and crisp, the preparation and distribution of such cards might even be a joint Protestant-Catholic effort, and the use of the cards a deepening of that "unity of hearts" which we all see with increasing clarity as an ineluctable demand of the Christian law. Such a suggestion may smack of the artificial, but it is no more so, I suspect, than was the classroom custom of recited prayer and Bible reading. In any case, we can no longer have the latter, and, if we are really concerned, might just as well try the former.

There are additional ways by which the legitimate concerns of religiously committed parents might be alleviated, but, again, most of these solutions have met with more of a ritualistic rejection than a realistic examination. Shared-time, for example, represents an effort to break out of the box which custom has built around the whole question of how and to what degree the sacral expectations of parents might be met by the public schools. Shared-time is not, obviously, a full and final answer to the misgivings of parents who feel that religious values are an integral part of education, yet cannot be inculcated in the public school; nor will shared time restore to peaceful nights those educators whose mystique of public education leads them to regard religiously oriented schools as divisive and alien to the spirit of a democracy. For anyone interested in resolving the present impasse, however, shared-time would seem to represent, not a course for immediate adoption, but an expedient deserving of serious study and open-minded exploration. There is, however, little evidence from the side of either Catholic or public school administrators generally that the question is a particularly live one among them.

A similar instinctual closing of the window when a fresh breeze is felt can be seen in the general failure of educators —in both public and church-affiliated schools—to ponder possible ways of exploring and perhaps implementing the dictum of Justice Clark in giving the majority opinion of the Court in the Bible reading case, a dictum which makes clear that the public schools may teach about religion, and present the Bible as literature and history. Justice Clark said in part: "It might well be said that one's education is not complete without a study of comparative religion or the history of religion and its relationship to the advancement of civilization. It certainly may be said that the Bible is worthy of study for its literary and historic qualities. Nothing we have said here indicates that such study of the Bible or of religion, when presented objectively as part of a secular program of education may not be effected consistent with the First Amendment." As in the case of shared time, Justice Clark's dictum will not satisfy the extremists on either side, but the dictum is certainly deserving of more than a ritualistic response.

Its value as a possible path out of a *cul de sac* can perhaps best be seen if we reflect on the creeping paralysis which characterizes the thought of educators concerned with the relation of public education to religion and spiritual values. The Supreme Court decisions in the McCollum case and Regents' Prayer case left many uncertainties as to what public schools were constitutionally permitted to do in dealing with values and religion. The American Council on Education, for example, which once had a Committee on the Place of Religion in Public Education, has entirely dropped its work in this field. The Religious Education Association felt a growing uncertainty about the same area from the McCollum case to the Prayer case—an uncertainty which has been dispelled, at least in the association's thinking, only by Justice Clark's dictum on the place of the Bible and religion in the public school curriculum.

Here, then, is another area in which Catholics might well make a distinct contribution to public education by evidencing their serious interest in exploring with other religious bodies and with school administrators the full implications and practical implementation of Justice Clark's statement.

It is deceptively easy to assail the Supreme Court's decisions in the prayer and Bible cases as a canonization of anti-theism and the erection of secularism into the *de facto* philosophy of public education. Christian spokesmen of different denominations have spoken loudly in this vein, and will probably do so again. More to the point, however, would be a mobilization of effort on the part of the religious community to discuss how the cloud of prevailing religious illiteracy of public education can be lifted without damage to constitutional limits or the delicate demands of religious pluralism.

Until American Catholics, in sufficient numbers and with the requisite authority, have made such efforts repeatedly and found them fruitless, we should cease decrying the "godlessness" of the public schools, and wringing our hands over their enforced secularism. The Good Samaritan bent to bind up his neighbor's wounds; he did not stand, in either dismay or exultation, counting and describing them.

To some Catholics, of course, as to some Christians generally, the public school will always be viewed as promoting a philosophy of secularism so long as some education toward religious commitment is not given, and moral-spiritual values not positively inculcated. Indeed, judging by the initial responses of some major Christian spokesmen to the Supreme Court's decisions, one might easily conclude that fear of secularism in the schools runs like a dye through the fabric of American Christianity.

This situation calls for a re-examination of what secularism actually is in the context of American pluralism. Certainly American Catholicism will contribute little to the constantly evolving ethos of America if whatever comes to it not clearly labeled religious is branded secularistic. Americans deserve better of us than an application to American realities of paradigms and thought models derived from European contexts or grown thin by transmission from the Middle Ages.

To begin, one must question whether, statistically at least, secularization has made the inroads into American life which some religionists claim. There are, for example, proportionately many more Americans affiliated with churches today than at the time of the Founding Fathers. In the narrow terms, only one-third of contemporary American Catholic adults have received any form of Catholic education, yet the level of Catholic practice among those same adults is the greatest in the world. The "secularism" of either American culture in general or public education in particular would seem at least no more corrosive than the cultural climate of Italy or Argentina, where secularism seems not looked on as a clear and present danger.

Beneath the statistics is a cultural fact to which Catholics have paid, perhaps, insufficient attention. As Karl Rahner, S.J., has pointed out, the rise of secularism is, in great part, not a moral or religious phenomenon but an intellectual one. In our day, Father Rahner points out, "the non-religious areas of existence in contrast with former times, have become of tremendous density, fullness, complication and capacity for absorption." Modern schools—and modern life—are inextricably involved with areas of decision and instruments of analysis unknown even a century and a half ago—sociology, anthropology, depth psychology, bio-chemistry, economic geography, technology, cybernetics, economic management, political science, to mention but a few of a long and growing litany of comparatively new and valuable areas of learning and life.

In the past, religion was often thought to hold the answers to the questions which these new disciplines have raised, and much of what might, at that time, have seemed absorption in religious thought evidenced defects of secular understanding rather than authentic religious inquiry into the macrocosm and microcosm. Religiously committed people of our day must be very careful not to confuse the growth of secular understanding with secularism. To do so would be to forfeit every effective chance to forge what the modern world needs and what Christianity—especially Roman Catholicism—can give—a theology of the temporal order. It is for contemporary Christianity to begin what previous generations of Christians could not possibly have done: to test the outer limits of what is usually dismissed as the secular order or the merely natural. Surely we cannot continue to view "the world" as, at best, the backdrop to the central drama of the individual's struggle to win salvation and, at worst, the booby-trapped universe through which the Christian pilgrim must carefully pick his way.

Indeed, the centuries-old image of the Christian should perhaps yield to another more relevant to our century. Again it is Karl Rahner who suggests what the new image might be. The present situation of Christians today, insists Father Rahner, is that of a diaspora. Almost everywhere the Christian, and *a fortiori* the Catholic, lives in a culture, a state, amid political and economic movements, artistic and scientific developments which are not conducted solely and simply for Christians or by Christians. The Catholic in this condition of diaspora will increasingly find his faith, if not threatened, at least not supported from without. His Catholicism will receive little assistance from institutional morality, conventional wisdom, custom, public opinion or public institutions.

Unlike the Christian of the Middle Ages, or the Catholic citizen of a "Catholic country," the Catholic in the diaspora cannot expect to derive spiritual sustenance from the structures of his culture. In the diaspora, he is expected to impart spiritual sustenance to these structures, rather than to draw it from them. Not a pilgrim between two worlds, but the Church at her frontiers in this one; such is the image of the Christian in our increasingly "secularized" world, in the diaspora.

Whether in Catholic or in public schools, the young Catholic students of today and tomorrow must be prepared to live in the diaspora. Recalling that millions of Catholics will receive some or all of their education in public schools, one can but note how such schools reflect in miniature the world of the diaspora into which *every* Catholic student will graduate.

This fact alone should make Catholic parents and educators aware of the strategic importance of public education on every level, and make them spend every effort to insure that the Catholic student in the public school be supported by every resource—spiritual, moral and financial —which American Catholicism can provide. There are still too many casually conceived C.C.D. programs, too much Catholic indifference to the financial, educational and religious needs of public education *in se,* too many dioceses which support the Newman Movement as a General Staff supports an army that it knows is trapped and doomed, too little readiness to try new possibilities or even to think new thoughts about public education.

I suspect that Catholic education will become increasingly an education for an elite—hopefully, an intellectual rather than a financial one. If this is the case, then we American Catholics cannot afford stereotypes in our thinking about either Catholic or public education. Indeed, the future of the Church in America in 2000 may well be principally determined by how we Catholics think about and act toward public education in the year of Our Lord 1964.

ROBERT T. FRANCOEUR

The Price We Pay

My twenty-six years on the student side of Catholic education have ranged from a small parochial elementary school, through an all boys high school, a men's college and on to graduate work in four other Catholic colleges and universities. Mingled with this work as a student have been varied experiences on the other side of the desk, teaching high school physics and chemistry in Detroit, biology and religion for four years in Steubenville, and then various biological courses at two Catholic colleges in the East. In the past three years, while continuing graduate work, my contact with secular education (and with Catholics in secular education) has been deepened by guest lectures and visits to non-Catholic universities and colleges in ten states and two countries. Such visits usually included an informal meeting and discussion with the faculty that brought opportunity for contact with a broad range of frankly expressed and sincere views on Catholic education. On such tours, I am more of an observer than a professional educator. This same observational role has been reinforced daily over the past six years by life in large and small parishes in the East and a small twenty-one family parish in the Ohio valley, at day by day meals with the superintendents of two diocesan school systems, and by simply listening to principals, teachers and administrators discuss their problems and labors casually at meals. All this has left me with some definite views on Catholic education, views which have been constantly tested and submitted to the acid criticism of those with much greater personal experience and involvement in Catholic education. These views, I feel, reflect not only my own personal appraisal, but are a synthesis of views expressed by Catholic and non-Catholic educators, and by parish priests from Arizona to North Dakota, Washington D.C., Pittsburgh, New York and Toronto.

A synthesis of views from across the country, such as I propose here, is a dangerous project, as is any generalization. But it is a synthesis that must be attempted, carefully calculating the risk, if we are to look below the surface problems of Catholic education today and touch the root of the real problem—the price we pay, not in money but in warping the true concept of Catholic education, the role of the Church as educator of all Catholics, and the function of the priest in the Christian community.

What I will attempt to present here, then, is the maturation of many views and conversations. It is a judgment and evaluation of Catholic education that is already quite widespread across the country and a view that is heard more and more from every quarter. Though the professional educator in the Catholic school may justly claim to be more at home in an evaluation such as I am presenting, it may be that freedom from the all-absorbing task of administration and teaching plus a wide contact with the educational scene across the country has allowed me the leisure necessary to appraise and compare my impressions with those of other teachers and students, with parish priests especially, as well as with educators in the non-Catholic areas. Though this background may not be, and is not, as broad as I would like it, I feel it is solid enough to act as a valid basis for some comments on Catholic education.

This kind of a detached survey can lead to a whole flock of questions about the problems of our Catholic schools. The immediately pressing one, of course, is the problem of the prudence, political and social, of pressing one's claims, in justice, for federal aid; or failing in this, the equally pressing one of where to get the necessary monies to continue financing the system. But well below these surface problems, other deeper ones have come to mind. These have to do with the problem of cost, but not in terms of dollars and cents—rather in terms of cost in a warping of attitudes: toward the Church, the priesthood, and the role of the parish in the life of the parishioners.

One would hope that many people acquire this leisure and freedom to examine our school system. One would like to see investigation of the problems of lay-clerical relations as affected by the schools, the development of a true instrument for measuring the academic value of our separate schools, an examination of the effect of the large private system upon the real work of the public school system, and a plumbing of the basic sources of the church-state tensions which are occasioned by our schools. Obviously, in an article of this size, I must leave most of these questions to others, limiting myself to the question of what our parish schools have cost our parishes.

I would like to ask what effect our concentration on the school has had on our understanding of the purpose of the Church, and thus of the true function of the parish; to inquire what this concentration on formal education has done to the practice of priesthood, and consequently to our understanding of the nature and function of priests. I would like, with great fear, to open the question of the effect of this school system on the religious life of our sisters, and to suggest the effect of the school-centered parish on the adults and on the very children of the parish.

To start our investigation, let us take a ride out through suburbia. Typically, on a choice corner lot there is a large plant: a very large school, of many classrooms. Somewhere in the middle of the L-shaped, or wing-shaped school, there will be an auditorium. This may or may not be visible from the highway. Near the school there will be a large, dormitory-style structure, whose cross identifies it as the convent. On the other side of the school there is a smaller building, partly a home, partly an office, which is the rectory. This plant is identified by a large sign as St. Somebody's Church.

And yet the passerby on the highway sees no church. We who are among the initiates know that the auditorium doubles as a church. We know that the church will follow in due course, as soon as the population increase permits.

Every day this plant, by its very existence and its function, teaches the pastor, the parishioners, the neighbors and the passersby that this is in fact St. Somebody's School. As far as signs go, as far as the visible element is concerned, the Catholic Church has been submerged into the Catholic school.

Parenthetically, it can be asked why we are surprised when our non-Catholic fellow citizen equates aid to our schools as direct aid to our Church. We have made him all too aware of the identification by our actions and by our very buildings, for the last half century or more.

The very size of this plant is the cause of many of the problems we are considering, so it might be well if we took a brief glance at our recent past to seek some explanation for this size of the American parish.

The present-day parish—with its thousands of members, its hundreds, or even thousands of grammar-school students, its large number of teachers and its priestly staff of several curates and a pastor—flows directly from a policy decision of the nineteenth century. The ideal of "every Catholic child in a Catholic school" was launched in a church which was understaffed with priests and poorly organized on the diocesan level. The practice grew of making parishes large enough to sustain an adequate school for the children of a neighborhood. Each parish had its own school and each school had its own supporting parish. It would be wrong of us to blame the men of those days for not seeing the value of central schools, under the control of a diocesan office of education, since there were no diocesan offices of education. These administrative devices are the creation of our own century. The idea of several small parishes, each with a limited number of families, each with only one priest, but all supporting a central school, just could not have occurred to anyone in those days.

The failure of our own century to grasp this fundamental shift on the administrative level is harder to excuse. The very race to keep up with the expanding number of children seems to have precluded any creative analysis of the basic structure. Certainly the mass migration to the suburbs that followed World War II could have been the occasion for such a fundamental shift. But unfortunately the opportunity was not seized. We went along, doing what had been done by our fathers.

After this all too brief look at history, let us now ask a few questions about what this large school-parish has done. How has this structure conditioned our way of thinking about the Church and about the real role of the parish?

In these days of the Second Vatican Council, when the Church calls us to re-examine all things in the light of essentials, can we honestly say that the average American Catholic really understands what the role of the Church is? Is that unfortunately typical pastor right who says, "You don't have a parish until you have a school"? Can a superintendent of schools be permitted to state that "this parish exists for its school"? Such statements show forth an abysmal confusion of means with ends. They point out a glaring lack of fundamental insight into the mystery which is the Church.

Even at this early date we have been given guidance by

the Second Vatican Council. In speaking of the liturgy the Fathers said, "While the Sacred Liturgy does not absorb all of the activity of the Church, it is nonetheless the goal towards which all of the activity of the Church strives, and it is the source from which all of the activity of the Church draws its strength." The medievalists couched it more succinctly: *magisterium propter sacerdotium,* teaching is for worship. If this is valid when we consider the very teaching office of the Church itself, how much the more should it be true when the teaching is on the level of grammar schools?

Yet when one compares the state of worship in the average American parish with the state of education, the comparison makes one wonder what has the primacy. The Eucharist is the Last Supper made present for this group of disciples of the Lord; it is the family meal of the Family of God. The distortion of Sunday Mass in the average American parish escapes us because we are so used to it—but ten or twelve Masses, rushed through to satisfy the demands of the parking lot can be labeled nothing short of an abuse. To see the abuse, all we have to do is try to imagine a family Thanksgiving Day dinner served in twelve shifts.

But the erosion has gone deeper. When we say formation, or education, in the American context, we think only of that type of education which is given to pre-adults. That the Church must teach and form her own, all during their lives; that the Church must speak to the developing needs of her members when they are thirty and forty and fifty, as well as when they are in their pre-teens; that the Church must speak, not only to the intellect, but to the whole person; that the Church has been given by Christ language and a means of formation that is apt for all and for all times: these truths are simply not recognized, so all absorbing have the demands of the school become.

This inability even to see that the essential function of

the parish is to raise up worshipers in spirit and in truth, is paralleled by a practical refusal to see what a priest is and what he is for.

The large school, living off a large parish, has led us to use priests in a most odd manner. Because of the haunting monarchic ideals of the past, our parishes are presided over by prince-pastors, who are assisted by men called priests, who are competent to judge the internal forum but who are allowed to have no real say in policy decisions. That most American pastors are benign, that most are conscientious is quite true. But it does not take away from the fact that a man does not reach this august state until twenty or thirty years of an apprenticeship that has not fostered, but if anything has depleted, any initiative he may have had. For all during this time, and during his time as a pastor, he must be primarily concerned with maintaining a plant. All of the details of money-raising and spending are the lot of the priests. The onus, as well as the responsibility, is his. The residue of European myths about money-grubbing clerics is developed in the real need to amass the monies necessary to maintain the large plant.

But beyond this, the very size of the parish makes it impossible for the priest to exercise any real pastoral care. The hundreds of families that make up the parish cannot possibly be the subject of pastoral visitation. When our Protestant brothers tell us about their exercise of the pastoral care, we can only look at them with envy for the freedom which is theirs to practice a real ministry.

When we note the absence of any impact by the parish on its neighborhood, perhaps the cause flows from this necessary concentration on parish-school needs, which blinds the priests to their responsibility to stir their people to civic action. Or perhaps it flows from an activism, almost endemic to Americans, which prevents the priests from keeping abreast of developments within the Church, even of the commands and exhortations of the modern popes.

Of course the priests are not the only religious specialists in the parish structure. There are also the teaching sisters. That the Catholic school system has been firmly rooted in the self-sacrifice of these dedicated women is becoming agonizingly clearer, as their diminishing numbers have to be replaced by lay teachers. But I think it can be at least questioned if we have not exacted from them an even higher price for their service to the parish school. This price may have been a confusion of a call to the service of God in religion with a vocation to be a teacher. The imperious needs of the Church called forth not only a large number of teaching orders (seventy percent of which have been founded since 1840), but it has almost equated a vocation to be a sister with a vocation to be a teacher.

Many a confessor, as well as many a parent, has been faced with the tragedy of a person who has no inclination, little taste, and small natural aptitude to teach, being forced into a lifetime of teaching. Only in the last few years have vocational directors raised the question of a natural basis for a vocation to a particular order. In the past, the natural, human attraction of a particular sister has been the basis for a decision to enter sister's order. The poor girl who faints at the sight of blood may well end up in a nursing order, and the girl with a natural bent for adults and a mild antipathy for children may end up teaching first-graders. Justice to the child and to the teacher are not served in such circumstances .

To assay the price our faithful have paid for the large school system, let us look first at the essential faithful: the adults of the parish. A parishioner who has children in the parish school is a parishioner whom the Church is consciously serving. Those parishioners whose children have grown, or who have no children, or who are not married, find themselves cast on the periphery of attention and occupation on the part of the parish, precisely because they are peripheral to the school. Here the question of a broader understanding of the word "formation" becomes pressing. Grant that the Faith is not something that is packaged and delivered in a developed state to a person either at baptism or at graduation, it becomes imperative that the parish realize it has a responsibility to aid in the developing faith of all its members. Pius XII said that one cannot solve a man's problems with a boy's knowledge, but a school-centered, child-centered parish has no concern for giving a man's knowledge to all its members.

This is not a call for a developed adult education program, because that would merely lock the parish in an even larger "educational" endeavor. But it is a call for a more mature understanding of the didactic function of the liturgy, for a real grasp, and thus use, of the formational capabilities of a worshiping community. When we grasp the fact that Christ is interested in the growth of all of His brothers and sisters, that He is concerned that they enter always more and more into the mystery, and that He has provided us with the means to do this, then we will be willing to give all of the adults the attention they need. The liturgy is naturally structured, as well as supernaturally endowed, to do this, because it appeals not only to the intellect alone, but to the whole man—not just once, but year in and year out.

Because the language of the liturgy is precisely that beautifully imaginative, pictorial language of the Holy Bible, it can speak to all manners of men. A biblical scholar, a harried housewife and a pre-schooler can all see and hear the signs, symbols and words of the liturgy, and each can be enriched, according to his own capacity and needs. Sermons which are couched in biblical language alienate no one. Hymns based on the psalter, when the psalter itself has been exhausted, are the natural hymnody of a Christian people. When the liturgy speaks of sheep and shepherd, of rocks and swords, of people in flight, of people at home, of houses built on sand or on rock, of sheep shorn and coats being shared, of miles being walked, it speaks to all men.

A man is still a member of the Church when his children have left the parochial school. He is still a member of Christ even if he has no children. And he should be treated as such by his parish.

Strangely enough, those very persons for whom the school exists, the children, have borne part of the cost of their schools. The little ones of the Lord have been asked to pay for their education by having lopsided parishes, school-centered priests, and a church which is merely the supporting device for their school. Because their parish is child-centered they are like the poor American child Harry Golden laments over, because he has nothing to grow up to. When the Catholic child finishes his Catholic grammar school he goes to a nearby Catholic high school or to the public high school. At this important moment of his life he finds that his parish has little more than a social program to offer him.

When he finishes high school, he may go on to college. If he goes to a Catholic college, he comes back to his parish and finds that it has nothing for him. If he goes to a non-Catholic college (and fifty percent of those who go to college do), he comes back, and tragically there is nothing for him. When he comes out of college and goes to work, there is nothing for him. All of the vast apostolic possibilities of his work, all of the rigorous demands made upon him as a now voting citizen—all of these cannot be the object of concern and action by his parish, because the parish is busy about the education of the children.

I must admit that these considerations seem to call forth rather dour and hard conclusions, but let us for a moment look at some of the opportunities they offer any one who has the courage to live like Pope John. For instance, the concentration of the priest on money. Here is a marvelous opportunity to call his laymen into consultation, and to give them real responsibility, not only for raising but also for spending the monies of the parish. Let him share his load, let him unburden himself so that he can be father to adult sons and daughters. Let them give him the leisure he needs to keep abreast of the Church so that he can lead them into the new era of the Church. Let them give him the freedom to be for them what Christ meant His priests to be.

Even if we have to accept the fact that larger numbers of our children will not be able to get into Catholic schools, this is no unmixed curse. A fine, fully developed C.C.D. program in a parish can call forth much more of the talent of the parish, can give a scope for many more of the adults, and can be a seed ground from which perhaps the parish lay boards of the future may grow.

Certainly, the least we can do is to plan for our future expansion. We can recognize that our situation is not the same as that of our fathers. We can take advantage of a higher degree of organization on the diocesan level. With this to take over the administrative burden of our schools we can plan new parishes, in the ever-expanding suburbs, that will be of a more manageable size. Parishes with a smaller number of families, with only one priest, can work in co-operation with other such parishes in the support of a central school.

We must ask all the questions that many educators and priests are asking today: Is it just to expend the labors of seventy-five or a hundred priests on the education of two or three thousand Catholic students on a sheltered college campus while next door one priest, often part-time, is reluctantly assigned to care for the spiritual education of hundreds and thousands of Catholic students on a state campus? Is it the mind of Christ that his priests and religious become so child-centered that their contact with adults in the parish is only seen in the light of the school? Is it Christ-like to ignore the formative and didactic elements of the liturgy and hand our adults the hollow shell of an unintelligible Sunday morning "rat-race" because of an infantile myopia or a parochial cataract that limits our vision of the Church? Can we continue to ignore the historical basis of our American parochial school system and the fact that the sociological milieu and need which brought that system into existence has disappeared before the more catholic concept of an adult-centered Church where the mission is to "teach all"? Can we continue to ignore the mind of the Church, expressed by the Council Fathers, on the Christian community fully committed to Catholic education as Christ intended it: the education of all Christians throughout their lives in the mystery of Christ, and their vocation to be his witnesses in the world?

Above all, if we take a realistic look (that is to say, a theologically and sociologically sound look) at the price we have paid for our schools, and refuse to pay this price in the future, we can remove any confusion of means with ends, of secondary things with the primary concerns. We can begin to do in our parishes what Pope John wanted to do for the whole Church.

When we know what our parish is, and what it is not; what our priests are, and are for, and what our sisters can be expected to do; when we unleash the powerful love and dedication of all our adults; when we let children be children in a adult world; then we can set about the proper business of the Church.

A. C. F. BEALES

Great Britain: England and Wales

Religious instruction in the schools of England and Wales is governed by the Education Act of 1944, which covered both kinds of school, the "county schools" of the local authorities (equivalent to the U.S. public schools) and the "voluntary schools" of the religious denominations. Under this Act the State is no longer neutral in religious education, as it had tried to be since 1870; for not only does the Act require a daily act of corporate worship in *all* schools, but it prescribes two periods per week of religious instruction in all schools. In the non-Catholic voluntary schools and in the county schools this religious instruction is in terms of an Agreed Syllabus, agreed to locally by the local education authority and the several religious bodies concerned (except the Catholics).

There are three kinds of voluntary (denominational) schools: "Aided"—where the school was able to find 50 percent of the necessary reorganization costs in 1944 and public money furnished the rest, the school then remaining fully and freely a denominational school as before; "Controlled"—where the religious body preferred to relinquish the school to the local authority, which itself thereafter paid the full cost of reorganization, but no longer with any guarantee that the *ethos* and the teachers would in the future be of the denomination which had created the school; and a few "Special Agreement" schools stemming from a previous Act in 1936.

The 2,000 or so Catholic schools in England and Wales reflect a history in which primary and elementary education is the heritage of the parish school (since before Catholic Emancipation in 1829) and secondary education is the heritage of the religious Orders. In 1944 the Hierarchy opted solidly for "aided" status for their schools; there is only one Catholic "controlled" school; and the "independent" schools of the Orders are increasingly becoming "aided"—a status which means that, once the half-cost of reorganization and extension has been found from private sources, the maintenance of the school is thenceforward financed completely from public funds, while the school remains fully Catholic in every way. By contrast, about half the Anglican schools (of the Established Church of England) have become "controlled," and practically all the schools of the Protestant Free Churches.

The Catholic population is usually considered to be one-tenth of the national population. But by 1970 the Catholic child population will be a substantially greater proportion than that. According to the calculations of the Newman Demographic Survey, the Catholic schools today contain some seventy percent of the Catholic child population; the rest are in county schools. This is due partly to shortage of schools and teachers, partly to parental complaisance. The urge to provide school-places for these other Catholic children has been stimulated by increased State building-grants (up to 75 percent of the cost in certain cases) under the Education Act of 1959, negotiated by Bishop Beck of Salford, Chairman of the Catholic Education Council for England and Wales.

There are two Catholic teacher training colleges for men, and ten for women. Several others are being created at this moment, as part of the national plan for educational expansion. These denominational teacher colleges receive 75 percent State-grant towards their building expansion, and a full 100 percent grant for maintenance. But Catholics who are university graduates, training for work in secondary grammar schools (U.S. senior high schools) are for the most part trained in the (secular) Education Departments of the universities. There is no Catholic university in England, and Catholic opinion is sharply divided on the desirability of one.

In short, then, the English situation is far removed from that of Australia, New Zealand and the United States, where denominational education receives no support from government funds. It is much nearer to that of Holland and Scotland, where religious education for every child, and of the kind demanded in conscience by the parents, is completely financed by public money.

The situation in Scotland today has been in force since the Education (Scotland) Act of 1918, the Act that contains (in Section 18) the world-famous "Concordat."

Scottish education rests on a foundation of Presbyterian parochial schools dating back to the seventeenth-century, with a Catholic parochial school development since Emancipation in 1829. This feature, together with the deep religiosity of the Scottish people, made possible in 1918 a real settlement of the Church-State question in popular education.

The local authorities wanted the *administrative* dualism (i.e. the coexistence of local authority schools and less-well-off denominational schools) abolished, in the interests of equal educational opportunity for all children. The religious authorities were favorable to this, but only if the *religious* dualism could be preserved, as something vital to them all. This the "Concordat" of 1918 contrived to do, by its provisions for the appointment of teachers. Applicants for teaching posts in a hitherto-denominational school were to be considered first by the religious authority concerned, which would draw up a short list of those religiously suitable. From this list the local authority would then appoint the applicant best qualified professionally.

In return for this explicit guarantee that the teachers appointed would be of the denomination that had created the school, and that it would continue of that denomination in its *ethos* and life, the religious bodies *sold* all their schools to the Scottish local authorities. In Scotland today, therefore, paradoxically, there are *no* denominational schools; all are local-authority-owned-and-financed. Yet all the religious bodies are satisfied, and the "Concordat" has behind it close on a half-century of successful working. Moreover, post-1918 new developments in education, such as Youth Organizations, have all come under the umbrella of the Concordat: so that each new step in the education of Scottish Catholics is similarly financed.

There are two Catholic teacher training colleges in Scotland for women, but none as yet for men. The bulk of Catholic teachers are trained in the secular teachers colleges, of which Scotland has five. These train both university graduates and non-graduates, for service in all kinds of schools. The university education of Scottish Catholics takes place in the four historic national universities, where the Catholic contribution, in seminars, etc., is substantial and valued, and where, as in England and Wales, the spiritual formation of the students is safeguarded by (increasingly resident) Catholic chaplaincies.

All in all, the treatment of religious education in Great Britain has suffered much less, in the post-war climate of secularity, than in many other countries. The historical explanation of this can be studied in Marjorie Cruickshank, *Church and State in English Education* (London: Macmillan, 1963). The working of the Agreed Syllabuses of Religious Instruction has been examined by the Institute of Christian Education—*Religious Education in Schools* (London: S.P.C.K., 1955). The situation as it affects the Catholic body is reviewed in the articles by Bishop G. A. Beck in the *Clergy Review* (London: Burns, Oates), *passim.*

GUNNAR D. KUMLEIN

Religious Education in Italy

There is a sad French saying, which occasionally can be heard in Italy too, and it runs as follows: the average Frenchman—or Italian—makes his first Communion in order to finish with religion, then he goes through high school in order to finish with his studies and finally he marries in order to finish with love.

However the situation may be as far as studies and love are concerned—the first part is in fact very often true. The religious ignorance of the Italians is in many cases such that it would make American Catholics shudder. It is a sort of widespread "religious infantilism" which has become even more pronounced since the pontificate of Pius X who, among other things, reduced the ages for first Communion from the earlier eleven to twelve years to seven or eight years. It is easier to remember what you learned at the age of eleven than what you learned at the age of seven.

From this point of view, the concordat between Italy and the Holy See, as far as religious education is concerned has only a relative importance. According to one of its paragraphs, in every high school there has to be at least one hour for the teaching of religion per week and roughly two hours per week in the elementary schools. Moreover, there are many Catholic schools and even Catholic universities in Italy, run by members of the orders or by secular priests; but they do not enjoy State support.

148

Roughly one out of every four Italian school children attends them. The issue does not disturb the excellent relations between Church and State and seems to be a *modus vivendi* which raises few objections.

It is therefore surprising that the results of the religious teaching are so poor. An increasing number of Italian priests have no doubts about the reason, recognizing humbly that partly the textbooks and partly the teachers themselves are responsible. The average religious textbook, still following the lines stemming from the time of Pius X at the beginning of the century, are written in such a way that they are largely incomprehensible to most of the children, mixed as the wording is with scholastic hairsplitting and strange old-fashioned theological expressions. The children learn these expressions by heart but have forgotten them six months later. First Communion becomes all too frequently a nice family feast with exciting new clothes for the child, his first wrist watch and all that, mixed with the tedious learning by heart by incomprehensible formulas. So, too, does the meaning of the Mass. This is all the religious "luggage" of innumerable adult Italians.

It has to be recognized, however, that a considerable effort has been made during the last ten years to make the Catechism more understandable to children, using graphics and illustrations and even the Montessori methods. Translations have been made from French, German and Dutch textbooks. But by and large the textbooks still used by most Italian children are as inappropriate as ever.

It has to be recognized here, too, that efforts have been made to improve the quality of the teachers: by training laymen and laywomen, for instance. Still, exceptional priests, particularly on the college level, confirm the rule that the average level is extremely low. The teachers of religion are generally not much better than the textbooks, be they secular priests or nuns.

Here the hopelessly backward training of the Italian seminaries comes into the picture, a training which is so inadequate to our times that already, over several centuries, a sort of negative selection has taken place within these seminaries. The best candidates have either fled to the orders or have been unable to resist returning to civil life. For that reason also the proportion of unfrocked priests in Italy is unusually high. The young priests brought out every year from the Italian seminaries have been compared to an army armed with bows and arrows against tanks and missiles. The formation of the nuns is even more narrow-minded and backward. The specific training of these teachers to teach catechism to children living in the world is surprisingly poor and inadequate too, be it for first Communion or in the elementary schools or high schools. Religion is therefore largely considered a matter which can be combed through in a hurry and soon forgotten.

It is therefore surprising that religion has survived as it has in Italy. Innumerable and faithful voters for Communism stick stubbornly to their religion in spite of their religious ignorance. Tests made in Southern Italy where the ignorance is greatest have shown that a surprising number of people do not hesitate to say that they believe firmly in God, at the same time as they can be strongly critical of the clergy. But their ignorance about the rest is such, it has been said, that if the Saracens returned to Sicily, for example, where they dominated for so long in the past, and turned the churches into mosques, the broad Sicilian masses would hardly be able to tell the difference.

All this is the consequence of the past or more precisely of "the counter-reformation complex" as many Italians would say, particularly now since Pope John's revolution.

The old structures are cracking everywhere and many bishops and particularly the younger clergy seem firmly determined to carry out that revolution to its last consequences. The boldest proposals are made for a drastic reform of all religious teaching, so that it hits children and adults alike. It is strange to say that TV has done a great deal to bring home to the broad masses that something has happened, watching as they have the Council in all its impressiveness and Pope Paul's pilgrimage to the Holy Land. The young clergy particularly is anxious not to be cheated anymore and anxious to receive, finally, arms more modern than bows and arrows.

A young parish priest in Rome said to me: "I have more than a hundred nuns in my parish. They are all of them saintly women, but their formation has made them useless for the essential tasks which are in front of me and which are tremendous. Do you know that only 14 percent of the Roman population goes to church regularly? We have to stick to essentials from now on," he continued, "talking about religious teaching and not lose our time with things like, for instance, the *pompa* in the Vatican which is out of date and even ridiculous, however glorious the tradition it stands for may be. . ."

DENIS O'BRIEN

Catholics and the Public School System in Canada

The general principle that in each province the Legislature shall make laws in relation to education, clearly stated in the British North America Act, has resulted in, not one, but ten education systems in Canada. The role of the federal government is restricted to the Territories directly under its authority, the education of Eskimos and Indians and families of members of the armed forces. In recent years, by agreement with the provinces, Ottawa has entered the education field with grants to universities but otherwise each province makes its own laws.

Because of this constitutional guarantee, policies and practices vary considerably. All provinces however are committed to the principle of a publicly-controlled, publicly-supported system, with compulsory education to age fifteen and free education to university entrance. Support comes from government grants and, except in the case of Newfoundland, local taxation.

The B.N.A. Act also guaranteed rights "acquired by law" in each province before entering Confederation. Prior to 1867, Catholics in Ontario had their own elementary schools; thus, while the Ontario Legislature may make the most revolutionary changes in the province's education system, it cannot abolish the separate (or Catholic) schools. Protestants in Quebec have the same constitutional guarantees. But in Manitoba, for example, Catholic schools were abolished in 1890: they existed prior to Confederation but had not been established by law.

About half of Canada's 8.5 million Catholics (1961 census) live in Quebec and are overwhelmingly French-Canadian. Quebec's 600,000 non-Catholics number only about twelve percent of the province's population whereas in no province do Catholics number less than twenty percent. In this brief summary only the most general observations can be made, but of Quebec it may be said that the province's generous treatment of its Protestant (and Jewish) minority is in sharp contrast to British Columbia's failure to recognize the rights of that province's 300,000 Catholics (22 percent of the population).

Quebec has a dual system of Education: the Protestant Education Committee is a completely autonomous body. However, education in French Canada is in for a drastic overhaul. The change will not affect the rights of minorities or alter the confessional character of the schools but it will give the Province a fully-integrated state system, under a Minister of Education, for the first time. The idea is to streamline and modernize the system, to give laymen and parents a more important role and to bring the system under government control. Higher education in Quebec is clerically-dominated to the point of suffocation and reactionary elements are vehemently opposed to any change. However, educational reform is basic to Quebec's quiet revolution and the idea is not to secularize the schools, to throw the cassock out of the classroom, but rather to adapt the system to the needs of today, for it is quite evident that the province's present medieval system is out of touch with the time; more pointedly, it is out of touch with the people.

The situation in the nine other Provinces can be summarized briefly as follows:

Ontario: Elementary Catholic schools with provision for education through Grade Ten under a system of government *Continuation* grants. The law states that Protestants *must* pay their school taxes to the public treasury while Catholics *may* support the Separate Schools. No provision is made for Catholic high schools, while Catholics must support the public high schools.

Manitoba: No Catholic schools since 1890—religious instruction is permitted during the last half hour of the school day.

Saskatchewan: Similar to the Ontario system with continuation grants through Grade Ten.

Alberta: Public-supported Catholic schools to university level. An important point is that Catholics must support their own schools, i.e., they may not pay their taxes to the public school treasury as in Ontario.

Newfoundland: The province brought its denominational school system with it when it entered Confederation in 1949. Catholics form about one third of the population and they operate their own schools as do the Anglicans and the United Church of Canada.

Maritime Provinces: In New Brunswick, Prince Edward Island and Nova Scotia there are no publicly-supported Catholic Schools except by "gentlemen's agreement" in some areas. But in the Maritimes generally, a liberal attitude towards religion in education keeps Catholics within the public school system. In New Brunswick and Prince Edward Island, convent schools, operated by nuns, are treated as public schools. In Halifax, Nova Scotia, Catholics organize and operate their own schools which are supported out of the public treasury under the city's famous gentlemen's agreement.

British Columbia alone among the ten provinces makes no concession to the conscience of Catholics.

Flexibility then is the characteristic Canadian approach to the question of religion in education. Although the various public school systems are non-sectarian they are by no means secular and in many provinces Bible reading and prayers are standard practice. There is no established Church in Canada or in any Canadian province but there seems to be general agreement that *separation* of Church and State does not mean *divorce*. Catholics labor under injustices and disadvantages in some provinces but they can always hope that a more enlightened government and public opinion will one day see the justice of their cause, since the principle of denominational schools has always been accepted in Canada.

ADOLPH SCHALK

Religious Education in West Germany and Austria

Before one can discuss religious education in West Germany, one must be aware of a fundamental difference in the Church-State relationship from that as we know it in the United States. The principle of strict separation of Church and State, which we hold so sacred, is completely foreign to the German mentality. To be sure, there is no such thing as a union of Church and State, and the two are indeed regarded as separate—but not separated—entities. Yet, although a State Church is strictly prohibited by the Basic Law (West Germany's constitution), Church-State agreements are intricately woven into the fabric of West German politics. For good or for ill, religion is not something outside of, apart from or in addition to German political life, but is constitutionally part and parcel of it.

Not only are the rights of the religious communities guaranteed by the Basic Law, which took over the provisions of the Weimar Constitution, but the religious bodies enjoy full legal recognition as statutory corporations. The autonomy of the Catholic Church is guaranteed by various concordats signed with the individual *Laender* (states) and on a federal level by the *Reich* Concordat, which was again recognized by the federal government after 1949. The Protestant group, which in Germany is composed predominantly of members of the Evangelical Lutheran Church, enjoys the same status as a result of historical developments, of the provisions of the constitutions and of various ecclesiastical contracts.

Not only is religious instruction in the public elementary schools recognized by the Basic Law and the state constitutions as a right, it is also regarded as a duty and is a compulsory part of the general curriculum, which in turn is subject to approval by the individual states, which have jurisdiction (rather than the federal government) over the German schools.

Every child registered as a member of a church is automatically required to take religious instruction and can only be exempted if his parents request it in writing; or, he can request the exemption himself after he has completed his fourteenth year. Religion instructors, whether priests, religious, ministers or lay persons, are a part of a school's regular faculty and receive a full salary from the particular state. In some states, notably Bavaria, pupils must take examinations in religion along with other subjects and can even be made to repeat the course if they flunk.

Thus, with some rare exceptions, two hours of religious instructions, built into the regular curriculum during normal school hours, are given weekly in the *Volksschule* (first four grades of elementary school) and three hours weekly in the *Mittelschule* (corresponding to the last grades of our grammar schools and/or the first two grades of high school). If the religion teacher is a priest or an ordained minister, he may even hold religious services or offer Mass in the school, and this is occasionally done. In some Catholic regions, a religious congregation may be in complete charge of a state (i.e., public) school, and receive their salaries from the state, which also pays for rent and repairs of the school building, if owned by the congregation.

As a result of this privileged position, the Churches in Germany have never regarded the establishment of separate parochial schools as a matter of great urgency, though some bishops and educators have been known to point to the United States' system of parochial schools as a model to emulate. Only about fifteen percent of West German elementary schools are private, and only a fraction of these in turn are strictly separate schools sponsored by the Church. In most cases they are boarding schools.

This system, however, is not quite as simple as it sounds. In most states, elementary schools are designated as *Simultanschulen* (i.e., "simultaneous" or common schools, attended by Catholics and Protestants alike). These pupils attend all secular classes together but are separated according to their confession for religious instructions, which are given in separate classrooms simultaneously. In addition, great attention must be paid to *proporz*, or the proper distribution of Catholic and Protestant teachers proportionate to the confessions of their pupils.

In areas that are predominantly Catholic or Protestant, however, the public elementary schools are designated as "confessional" and are run along strictly Catholic or Evangelical lines, depending on the confessional majority of the given neighborhood. Thus in a predominantly Protestant area, the schools might be Protestant-orientated, though even here they are obliged by law to admit Catholic pupils (in some places the number is limited by quota) and to arrange for Catholic religious instruction for them. And of course the same holds true for Catholic "confessional" schools.

Although the majority of elementary schools in West

Germany are *Simultanschulen,* in some states confessional schools predominate. Bavaria's public elementary schools, for instance, are about sixty to seventy percent confessional.

A widespread controversy has been raging for some time over the question of whether to do away with confessional schools altogether. Strongly influenced by the ecumenical spirit of the Council, many educators, Catholic and Protestant, urge that the *Simultanschulen* are more in keeping with interfaith harmony. But there are strong factions, who also draw their inspiration from the Council, who maintain that only in confessional schools can religion be properly integrated throughout the curriculum, and that this system in the long run will contribute more toward interfaith understanding. The *Simultanschulen,* they claim are neither fish nor fowl, only heighten the differences, and will ultimately cause friction.

A very important consideration in the German school question, especially as it affects religious instruction, is the fact that West German christians, whether Catholic or Protestant, support their churches by means of a special church tax collected by the government, which in turn distributes the money to the church authorities. It generally works out to ten percent of their regular income tax and accounts for about one percent of the average man's total income. Any West German who decides he no longer wishes to pay the tax must go before a local court and sign a statement that is tantamount to apostasy. Even though vast numbers of nominal church members do not go to church, it is estimated that no more than five percent of the population has declared itself churchless in order to avoid paying the church tax. Thus the Church has funds also for its private schools, which nevertheless receive partial subsidies from the individual states.

As a result of all this, religious education does not impose the staggering financial burden on the Church in Germany that it does in the United States.

The Austrian situation is very similar to the German, but not quite identical. Here there is a special law, *Religionsunterrichtsgesetz,* which requires religion to be taught in all public schools. If a child wishes to be dispensed from such instruction, his parents must request this in writing within ten days after the first day of school. After the age of fourteen the child can request the dispensation himself. Less than one percent of the children, however, have applied for this exemption, whether by themselves or through their parents. In vocational schools, however, religious instruction is optional.

Oral examinations in religion are given regularly and the pupils can be made to repeat a course if they flunk. Two hours of religious instruction as stipulated by law are given weekly in the public elementary schools. Religion textbooks must be approved by the state, and religion instructors are paid salaries by the state.

The Church in Austria is financed by an arrangement called *Kirchenbeitrag,* which is a kind of modified tax less strict than its German counterpart. The state, which is nominally ninety-five percent Catholic picks up the tab for sixty percent of the expenses incurred by private Catholic (i.e., parochial) elementary schools. This arrangement is a compromise with the socialists, who are opposed to Catholic private schools. Since thirty-three percent of all elementary schools are Catholic-sponsored, their sudden closure would create a national crisis.